MONUMENTAL DOGS

MONUMENTAL DOGS

The Amazing Stories
That Inspired People To Erect
Lasting Tributes
To Our Special Canine Friends

by

EDWARD SUMPTER

Requests for permissions should be mailed to:
Kookie Press
P.O. Box 1060
Sequim, WA 98382
www.monumentaldogs.com

ISBN-13: 978-1481229197

ISBN-10: 1481229192

Book and cover design: Magdalena Bassett, www.bassettstudio.com

This book is dedicated to my family; my loving wife Kathrin, my children Sam and Angela, my granddaughter Ava and all the dogs that have made my world a better place to be: Dinah Dog, Sugarfoot, Geeta, Kookie, and our current 'Best Friend in Training,' Chief.

AVA GRACE WEST AND CHIEF.

Introduction

*W*elcome to my book. Over the years I have been collecting interesting stories about dogs. Since many people I knew had never heard some of these great tales, I decided to gather the dogs up, put them in the kennel (this book) and share them with the world. There are so many to tell about, but for this collection I narrowed them down to a few of my favorites.

Facts are much more interesting than fiction and these stories show that to be true. When you read about the exploits of Bobbie who traveled over 2,500 miles across the country to return home, Igloo who provided much needed companionship, Rin Tin Tin who entertained millions, Swansea Jack who rescued scores of people from certain death, and the others, you realize that truth is the spark that brings a story to life.

As you read about these "Monumental Dogs," you will grow a little closer to your own furry friend. Your dog is a reflection of you; in a sense you build your own dog. The way we treat them, the patience we demonstrate and the love we bestow, all contribute to our dog's personality. I fondly remember the first dog in my life. Our family pet, 'Dinah', was no particular breed, just a medium sized brown dog. As a young child I remember playing with her and being able to crawl all over her with no complaint. She was part of the family. There have been many good dogs since. It seems their only fault is that they don't live longer.

The role of the dog in our lives has evolved dramatically. We have modified and refined them physically and mentally to fit our changing needs. Thousands of years ago our partnership was about mutual survival. Wolf and Man slowly grew closer and closer and evolved into a working team. The early tribes of hunters who lived and worked with dogs were the people who survived. It was the extra edge they needed in a harsh, unforgiving environment. To an Eskimo in the frozen north, a dog's sense of smell could mean the difference between a successful and unsuccessful hunt, between life and death. As Man evolved into an agrarian lifestyle our dogs adapted their role to become guardians and shepherds. Time marches on, society has become more complex and dogs have expanded their role accordingly. They now guide the blind, perform search and rescue, march with us to war, help the sick, entertain us, guard us in our homes and most importantly, provide companionship in a crowded but lonely world. They wait faithfully and grieve for us when we are gone. Rich or poor, through thick and thin they yearn to be with us, and that feels good. They always have been and still remain man's best friend. So get yourself comfortable, and with your best friend by your side, enjoy the book.

TABLE OF CONTENTS

GREYFRIARS BOBBY

Let his loyalty and devotion be a lesson to us all

This is dog-lover gold. The hero of our story is a "wee" terrier who became known as Greyfriars Bobby. The setting is the charming City of Edinburgh, Scotland, in the year 1853. John Gray or "Auld Jock" as he was known had come to town from the surrounding countryside looking for work. Despite his advanced age he was lucky enough to find employment as a constable for the city's police force. Because the police force had been originally founded by Sir Robert Peel, constables were nicknamed "Peelers" or "Bobbies," a name still heard today.

Jock and the other constables were required to have a dog to accompany them on their rounds, which was often all through the night. An important part of their job was to watch over the town's livestock. A dog's keen sense of hearing and smell were very helpful in alerting the officers to varmints (both the four and two legged

SKETCH OF BOBBY

Gift of Mrs. Riddell in memory of Peter Fletcher Riddell

varieties) and in helping to catch or scare them away. When Jock acquired his puppy, probably in 1856, his family found it fitting to give the young dog the name Bobby.

He was a Skye Terrier. This breed of scrappy furry dogs is known for their keen sense of smell, which enables them to find their prey even through several feet of soil. In fact, the name "terrier" finds its roots in the Latin word for earth, "terra." Although small, they are fierce and tenacious.

Auld Jock and Bobby patrolled the neighborhood known as Cowsgate, located in the old city, on the rougher side of town. The place had earned its name because of the nearby gate, which was a passageway through the old city walls. Livestock could pass through from the safety of their nighttime shelter, into the surrounding countryside, to graze during the day.

Lying in the shadow of Edinburgh Castle, the area featured the centuries old Greyfriars Church. Alongside the church, the Kirkyard (churchyard) contained the cemetery. Nearby was the Grassmarket, a large field which had been set aside as a permanent marketplace by James III during the 15th century. Jock and Bobbie's beat was the gathering place for an interesting mix of highlanders, shepherds, military personnel, fishmongers, pickpockets and thieves. They came to the vibrant neighborhood to enjoy the market, and to do business in the many pubs, cafes, shops and other area businesses.

As a perk of the job, Jock and his family were given a place to stay in his assigned neighborhood. Despite Jock's wife's misgivings about the location, it was required that a constable live where he worked. This policy wisely allowed the officer and the citizens he policed to become familiar with each other.

Auld Jock and his faithful companion would patrol all through the night. They would regularly stop in at the local businesses along their beat, including the many cafes and coffeehouses. Bobby became well known, made friends, and looked forward to the water, treats and attention he received. Being a policeman was a hard job. The combination of the damp cold air, pollution from coal smoke and the unsanitary conditions of the times took a toll on Auld Jock. He eventually became very ill, probably from tuberculosis. Too ill to keep working he was forced to stay at home to try and recover. After a few months, with his loyal canine friend and his loving family by his side, he died.

Bobby mournfully followed along as his master was laid in his coffin and taken away. Jock was laid to rest in the cemetery at Greyfriars Kirkyard. The next day, after the burial, the caretaker of the cemetery, Mr. Brown, found Bobby lying on the fresh earth of Auld Jock's grave. Bobby was shooed away but the next morning he was found asleep on the grave again. The Kirkyard had a strict rule against allowing dogs on the premises. The caretaker took his job seriously and sent the dog away again and again. But Bobby always found a way to sneak back in and hide near the grave.

Touched by the dog's desire to be close to his late friend the caretaker eventually allowed him to stay and keep his vigil. He and his wife even started feeding and taking care of the orphaned dog. Bobby earned his dinner by keeping children, cats and other unwanted visitors away from the grounds. He would sometimes wander the neighborhood but stayed close by and would always come back to his new home to sleep on or near the grave. The nearby tablestone monuments provided Bobby with shelter from heat, wind, and rain. During the following years many people in the neighborhood became part of his life. He made many friends who would give him food and shelter during cold wet weather.

Whenever he wandered outside the Kirkyard, he was a favorite playmate of the local children. They would run around together, play and enjoy each other's company. He would also visit area merchants who knew the dog's story and helped out when they could. One particular eating house that Bobby had previously frequented with his master became his favorite place to go. Successive owners of the establishment all fed him when he came to visit. Eventually the eating house was owned by John Traill, run by his family and was known as Traill's Temperance Coffee House. Bobby became closely attached to the Traill family. Mr. and Mrs. Traill had two children, Elizabeth and Alexander. He spent a lot of time playing with them and enjoyed their attention but he always returned to the Kirkyard and his master.

A frequent visitor to the Coffee House was Sergeant Scott of the Royal Engineers who was stationed at the Edinburgh Castle. To help make sure that the many clocks in the city were set to the same hour, it had been decided to signal the town from the Castle, at an agreed upon time. At first the time-signal was a large canvas ball that would slide up and then drop down the mast atop Nelson's Monument on the Calton Hill. This would allow ships anchored in the Firth of Forth to see the ball drop and set their clocks accordingly. Later it was decided to also fire a cannon so people could hear what time it was. The Sergeant sometimes took Bobby out for walks and up to the Castle where the gun was fired at precisely 1 o'clock every day (except Sunday). Since the good Sergeant would also feed him, the sound of the cannon fire became Bobby's daily signal that it was time to eat.

Once Bobby was picked up by the dogcatcher and was in danger of losing his life after being branded a stray. He needed a license and someone had to pay for it. The Lord Provost of Edinburgh, Sir William Chambers (who was also a director of the Scottish Society for the Prevention of Cruelty to Animals), felt sympathy for the scofflaw and came to the rescue. He paid what was due and took responsibility for Bobby's future license fees. He even had him fitted with a nice leather collar that identified him, and kept him out of future trouble.

The story of his brush with the law and the loyalty that kept him from leaving his dead master's grave was reported in the newspapers. Bobby's story was widely discussed and he had become a local celebrity. Crowds would gather and line the path outside the Kirkyard

THE TRAIL FAMILY WITH BOBBY. MR. & MRS. TRAIL, ALEXANDER & ELIZABETH ANN

Edinburgh Museums & Galleries: The Museum of Edinburgh

gates. They would wait to see Bobby make his short journey to the Coffee House for his daily supper after the cannon was fired. The groundskeeper would open the gate and Bobby, ignoring the crowds, would head off to eat. Many people also came to photograph, paint and sketch the famous dog. One sentimental and aristocratic visitor was Baroness Burdett-Coutts; she had read about the loyal dog in the newspapers and came to see for herself if the story was true. Sure enough she found him lying on the grave.

Bobby continued his vigil and his daily visits with his friends and admirers. His graveside vigil continued for an incredible 14 years. He died quietly of old age in Traill's home on January 14, 1872. Dogs were not allowed to be buried on the consecrated ground of the cemetery, so Bobby was buried just outside the Kirkyard, as close as they could put him, to be eternally near his master.

People wanted a reminder of the dog and a beautiful monument to Bobby was erected shortly after his death. The red granite fountain at the top of Candlemaker Row and near the George IV Bridge was donated by his admirer, the Baroness, and was unveiled November 15, 1872. It features a life size bronze statue of Bobby on the top.

In the middle is a drinking fountain for the public and near the bottom is a water trough for dogs. It is a beautiful monument and is a well-known tourist attraction today. A plaque attached to the fountain reads:

A tribute to the affectionate fidelity of Greyfriars Bobby. In 1858 this faithful dog followed the remains of his master to Greyfriars Churchyard and lingered near the spot until his death in 1872.

With permission erected by Baroness Burdett-Coutts.

Red granite headstones mark the resting places of John Gray and Bobby his loyal companion. John's reads:

STATUE AT JUNCTION OF GEORGE IV BRIDGE AND CANDLEMAKER ROW

John Gray Died 1858
'Auld Jock'
Master of "Greyfriars Bobby"
And Even in His Ashes Most Beloved

Erected by American Lovers of 'Bobby'

Nearby is Bobby's headstone. It was erected by The Dog Aid Society of Scotland and unveiled by the Duke of Gloucester on May 13, 1981. It is located near the entrance to Greyfriars Church, the inscription reads;

Greyfriars Bobby
Died 14th January 1872
Aged 16 years
Let his Loyalty & Devotion
Be a Lesson to Us All

There are scores of books, films, and articles about Greyfriars Bobby. A well-read book was written by Eleanor Atkinson and published in 1911. Each story puts a little different spin on the facts. But the various versions all have one common denominator, a loyal dog whose love of his master was so strong that even death could not break the bond, which is indeed a great story worth repeating.

Walt Disney made a movie in 1961; it was filmed on location and was very popular. I remember seeing it as a child and loved the story. As with many Hollywood productions some liberties were taken with the story. Rightly called a "semi-historical" anecdote, the movie did acquaint millions of people with Bobby.

Bobby's collar is still on display today at the Huntly House Museum in Edinburgh. It has a brass plate on it that reads **'Greyfriars Bobby from the Lord Provost, 1867, Licensed'**. Also on display is the metal dish given to him for his meals by John Traill. It is engraved **'Bobby's Dinner Dish'**. John Traill's eating house is now known as

GREYFRIAR'S CHURCH & BOBBIE'S HEADSTONE

©Peter Stubbs www.edinphoto.org.uk

GREYFRIARS BOBBY'S HEADSTONE

Above: BOBBY'S MONUMENT

©Peter Stubbs www.edinphoto.org.uk

Right: TOP OF MONUMENT

Photographer: Michael Reeve

Greyfriar's Bobby Bar. It is located near the famous fountain and statue.

On January 14, 2011 to mark the 150th anniversary of his death, the One o' Clock Gun & Time Ball Association held a ceremony and laid a wreath at Bobby's gravestone in front of Greyfriars Church. The chairman of the association dressed as Colour Sergeant Scott, the Royal Engineer who befriended Bobby and fed him. Bombardier Blue is a Yorkshire Terrier who represented Bobby at the ceremony.

So he is still there, buried close to his master's grave. It is an interesting story that everyone should hear. New research and facts continue to shed light on some of the details, but it remains a very inspirational tale that the inhabitants of Edinburgh and dog lovers everywhere enjoy telling. He is one of the city's most famous inhabitants and demonstrates the love our dogs are capable of.

THE CHAIRMAN OF THE ONE O'CLOCK GUN & TIME BALL ASSOCIATION AND
BOMBARDIER BLUE PUTTING WREATH ON BOBBY'S GRAVE. JANUARY 14, 2011

©Peter Stubbs www.edinphoto.org.uk

CHAPTER 2

BARRY DER MENSCHENRETTER

'The Lifesaver'

You have probably seen the iconic picture of the Saint Bernard dog, with a small barrel of liquor around his neck, rescuing freezing wilderness hikers. Perhaps in a cartoon or maybe a movie, the giant dog bounds through the snow and provides warmth and nourishment to the wayward traveler. The part about the barrel may or may not be true, but in this case the rest of the story lives up to the myth. The real life adventures of Barry, the most famous of these dogs, demonstrate the heroic heart inside these gentle giants.

Our setting is a winding path through what is now called the Great St. Bernard Pass high in the Pennine Alps between Italy and Switzerland. The path leads from the Valley of Aosto, Italy, to the Swiss Canton of Valais. It has been used as a trail through these rugged mountains since ancient times. In 218 BC, this strategic route was taken by the great Carthaginian General Hannibal on his amazing

"St. Bernard's to the Rescue"

Artist: John Emms

journey towards Rome during the Second Punic War. In the year 43 AD, the Emperor Claudius widened and improved the existing path to accommodate carriages and ox-drawn carts. It was then given the status of a Roman Imperial Road. At the highest point in the pass they also built a "mansio" and a temple in honor of Jupiter.

Time marched on and the power and organization of Rome dwindled. But the road they left behind remained as a necessary route for travelers crossing the Alps. Over the following centuries it was in constant use, especially by French and German pilgrims on their way to Rome.

In the beginning of the 11th century the Augustinian monk Bernard de Montjoux devoted himself to the spiritual life of the inhabitants of the Alps. He spent over 40 years preaching and converting in the area. During that time he founded a hospice and monastery at the summit of the pass along the old road. The monastery was built on the site of the now crumbling Roman temple. By the 16th century the names St Bernard Pass and St Bernard Monastery were in use. Bernard was canonized by the Church in 1681, and in 1923 St. Bernard was confirmed, by Pope Pius XI as the patron saint of mountaineers, skiers and the Alps.

Over the next few centuries, the monks and the monastery staff assumed the mission of looking out for travelers, providing food and shelter, and acting as guides. The topography and harsh climate created a motivation for the monks to get help for this difficult task.

Sometime between 1660 and 1670 the monastery started to acquire dogs to assist them with their mission. To help them with the physically demanding work, they slowly developed a breed of big strong dogs that was able to meet the physical challenges they faced. They were bred from the descendants of the Roman's Mastiffs and other local mountain dogs gathered from the neighboring valleys. These specially trained assistants would accompany the monks, and with their large broad chests help clear a path through the deep snow. Strong and intelligent with an extraordinary developed sense of smell, uncanny sense of direction, and resistance to cold, these large furry dogs were able to face the freezing winters and come to the distressed travelers rescue.

Perched high in the Alps at an elevation of over 8,000 feet, this long and windy pass presented travelers with deep snow and avalanche conditions much of the year. Steep and treacherous terrain created dangerous conditions that caused injury and took many lives. In the centuries before modern roads, communication and technology, travelers risked their lives making this long journey. When people became lost or injured the monks made it their job to search and rescue the victims. The monastery became well known for its generous hospitality and its special dogs.

From each litter, the most promising puppies were selected for the rescue work. The monks took them out and trained them how to search for and care for victims of avalanches. Eventually the dogs went out by themselves. They had learned how to travel in small groups and look for victims to rescue. Incredibly, the dogs worked as a team and when a person was found in need or unconscious, the dogs licked their face to rouse them and then one would use his body to warm the victim. If the rescued man was able to walk, the dogs would guide him to the monastery. If he was too weak they would drag him as far as they could and, either bark until a monk arrived, or return to the monastery to get help.

In 1800 a puppy was born that would eventually stand out from all the others. He was named Barry in honor of the monastery's founder, St. Bernard. Barry lived from 1800 until 1814. In his lifetime he reportedly saved over 40 people from death. His keen sense of smell allowed him to find buried victims, dig them out and assist in keeping them warm until rescued. While it is debatable about whether or not he wore a barrel around his neck, especially one containing brandy, it makes sense that some rescue items such as food and a blanket might be tied to the dog for the victims comfort.

These monks and their dogs saved thousands of lives by locating victims, digging them out and guiding them to safety under the harshest of conditions. It was very dangerous work. Many monks and dogs lost their lives trying to help stranded victims. It is estimated that over the years, the dogs helped save more than 2,000 distressed travelers. When Napoleon crossed the pass with his army of over 250,000, many lives were saved by the monastery and their great dogs. The stories spread across Europe and the monks and their dogs became well known for their protection of travelers.

One famous story is that a mother and her young child became lost and trapped in the snow. Barry went out to search and disappeared overnight. The monks were very worried when he did not return. Many dogs lost their lives on these dangerous missions. Barry showed up the next day with the child tied around his body with the mothers shawl. The story goes on to say that the child survived and was returned to the grateful parents. Barry was a hero.

Stories such as this were widely circulated and helped contribute to Barry's eventual worldwide fame. There do not seem to be many surviving records or details of his exploits. A fire at the monastery destroyed many records. One thing for sure is that Barry was a remarkable dog. He rescued many people and left a lasting impression. His story and fame has continued to this day.

After his death in 1814, the story and popularity of Barry inspired many poems, books, and paintings. He is honored at the famous Cimetiere des Chiens (Pet Cemetery), near Paris, France. It is located in Asnieres-sur-Seine, alongside the river. Visitors are greeted by the large centrally located monument that was erected in 1880. With the hospice in the background, it depicts Barry rescuing a small child who is riding on his back. Interestingly he has a gourd around his neck, not a wooden keg.

The inscription on the monument reads as follows:

Il sauva la vie a 40 persones
Il fut tue' par le 41 eme
Translated as: *He saved 40 people, killed by the 41st.*

"Napoleon Passing the Great St Bernard Pass"

Artist: Edouard Castres, Photographer: Ramas

MONUMENT AT ASNIERES-SUR-SEINE PET CEMETERY IN PARIS.

There are several variations but there was a story that while Barry was attempting to rescue an unconscious victim, (his 41st save), perhaps a soldier or maybe a criminal, he was mistaken for a wolf or an aggressive dog and he was fatally stabbed. It is now agreed that the story is not true, and that in fact Barry spent the last few years of his life in Berne, where he died peacefully, and of natural causes in 1814. After his death, his body was given to the care of the Berne Natural History Museum, where it remains to this day. The preserved body of Barry is now almost 2 centuries old. Currently he stands at the center of a special exhibit where he and his story still inspire people today.

Before the dogs were called Saint Bernard, they were referred to as Alpine Mastiffs, Hospice dogs, or Barryhunds (Barry dogs) in honor of the one special dog that stood out from the rest. Compared to the breed today Barry was smaller in size, with shorter reddish brown and white fur and a longer tail among other differences. In 1880 the Swiss Kennel Club officially recognized the name of St Bernard.

The breed has changed since Barry's time. Barry probably weighed less than 100 pounds whereas in the modern version a male dog can weigh up to 220 pounds. With their heavy fat and double thick fur coat this giant breed loves cold winters and cool summers. They have earned their reputation as one of the friendliest and most protective of man's best friends.

Until recently the Hospice at the Great Saint Bernard Pass still bred the famous name-sake dogs. The breeding program has now been turned over to The Foundation Barry du Grand Saint Bernard with kennels in Martingny, a village down the pass. Also in Martingny, and open in 2009, is located The Saint Bernard Dog Museum. The famous and popular dogs still return to the Hospice in the summer to the delight of dog lovers and tourists. In honor of the past, they always have one in the kennel they call Barry.

As far as the barrel around the neck controversy, many people doubt that the rescue dogs ever carried them. They are not mentioned in the monastery records, and it is pointed out that alcohol is probably the

BARRY EXHIBIT AT BERN NATURAL HISTORY MUSEUM

©Natural History Museum Bern

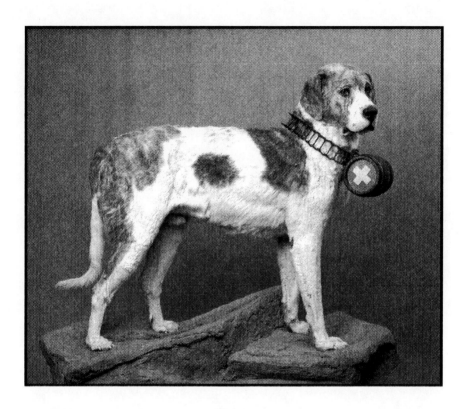

BARRY

worst thing for someone suffering from hypothermia. If it is a myth, it may have started when a barrel was pictured hanging on a dogs neck during a rescue in a famous painting, "Alpine Mastiffs Reanimating a Distressed Traveler," by Edwin Landseer in 1820. Historians also find it mentioned by a 17th century hiker who wrote, "Often the dogs receive a little barrel around their neck with alcoholic beverages and a basket with bread."

When originally preserved, and for many years there was no barrel around Barry's neck. The barrel was added in 1923, at the same time that Barry's aging body was restored and slightly modified to match the shape of the breed at that time. In 1978, Professor Walter Huber, the Berne Museum director, had his doubts about the historical accuracy of the attached barrel. He had it removed in his attempt to set the record straight. It has since been returned, and is in place today. Whether the barrel story is a myth or not, one thing is clear, it is indeed part of the story and the legend.

The search and rescue dogs have now been replaced with modern devices. Helicopters are much more efficient and cost effective. Yet Barry lives on, fittingly, a modern day avalanche rescue beacon now being manufactured and used around the world is known as a "Barryvox," Barry's voice. This one dog, Barry "the Lifesaver" Saint Bernard, was a special dog and his memory lives on.

THE MODERN ST. BERNARD

CHAPTER 3

SERGEANT STUBBY

It's not the size of the dog in a fight, It's the size of the fight in the dog.

—Mark Twain

The story of this little dog proves that heroes come in all sizes. One day in the spring of 1917, a small homeless puppy wandered onto the Army training field at Yale University in New Haven Connecticut. In the next few years he would march off to war, save lives, fight battles and be the most decorated dog of WWI. He would also become the only dog to be promoted to the rank of Sergeant through combat.

Stubby was a mixed breed of Bull Dog and probably Staffordshire Terrier mixed with Boston Terrier. He was a small brindle colored dog with white markings. Whatever breed of dog he was, he would prove that he had what it took to be a tough soldier. He was adopted by Private John Robert Conroy, who nicknamed his new friend 'Stubby" because of his short tail. Stubby's military career had begun. He proved to be very intelligent and was soon marching with the

STUBBY IN UNIFORM

Armed Forces History: Smithsonian Institution

men and he even learned the drills and bugle calls.

The World War or Great War as it was known (not called World War I until 1939), started July 28th, 1914. The United States entered the war as a self-described 'Associated Power', and joined the Allies "over there" in April, 1917. Fighting against the Allies were the Central Powers, which included Germany. Private Conroy was a soldier with the 102nd Connecticut Infantry, 26th Division. Formed in 1917 this Division consisted of units from the New England area and adopted the name "Yankee Division."

The men (and Stubby) of the Yankee Division were shipped overseas to France to fight as part of the American Expeditionary Force (A.E.F.). The men smuggled Stubby aboard the SS Minnesota and hid him in the coal bunker until they were out to sea. Stubby quickly endeared himself to the ship's crew. While on board, the ships machinist mate made Stubby his own metal 'dog tags', which he wore around his neck just like the rest of the guys. It is reported that when eventually discovered by the Commanding Officer, Stubby was allowed to stay with the men after he surprised the officer by giving a snappy military salute with his paw.

Once in France, the Yankee Division was sent to the front lines. Stubby was given a pass and allowed to accompany the men as their official mascot. They reached the trenches and joined the fight in February, 1918. Stubby soon adapted to the loud gun and artillery fire. During the hard fought war, Stubby and his comrades would be involved in four major offensives and 17 battles.

Stubby helped save lives by serving as a sentry and alerting the troops when his keen sense of hearing detected incoming artillery. After suffering injury from a previous gas attack, Stubby could sense it coming before the troops, and warned them beforehand, giving them time to put on their masks and thereby saving many lives. The men even fashioned their canine companion his own gas mask for protection. He helped to stand guard and had the ability to detect and find wounded soldiers in the dangerous, cratered, "no man's land."

Sometimes Stubby led them or even helped drag them back to safety. It was reported that he could find them by hearing which soldiers yelled for help in English, and then led rescuers to them. One report said Stubby helped carry messages between soldiers, even running under machine gun fire as he went.

During the raid on Schieprey, Stubby was injured by an exploding grenade. While recovering he helped lift morale at the Red Cross field hospital by visiting other wounded soldiers. During the battle of the Argonne he is credited with finding and capturing an enemy spy that he heard while on reconnaissance. Hearing him speak German, Stubby found and attacked what he knew was an enemy soldier. Grabbing his prisoner by the seat of his pants, he bit hard and did not let go until help arrived. For this deed Stubby was officially promoted to the rank of Sergeant by the Commanding Officer. He was the first dog to be given rank in the U.S. Armed Forces.

After the capture of Chateau-Thierry, the grateful mademoiselles of the area made Stubby a custom fitted chamois blanket-coat, embroidered with the flags of the allies. Over the years it was adorned with scores of Stubby's badges, buttons, awards and medals. At Neufchateau, the home of Joan d'Arc, he was presented with the first of his many medals. Stubby would continue to be honored with many more decorations that he would proudly wear on his jacket including, the French Medal Battle of Verdun, the St Michel Campaign Medal, the Chateau-Thierry Campaign Medal, and the Republic of France Grande War Medal. He also found room to hang his three Service Stripes, Yankee Division Patch, and his Wound Stripe (later known as the Purple Heart when introduced in 1932). Stubby even hung the Iron Cross Medal, taken from the captured German spy, near his tail.

Stubby and the Yankee Division spent 9 months fighting their way through France and into Germany. Every soldier needs and deserves a little down time, and Stubby occasionally went on leave and was seen in many French towns including Nice, Paris, Monte Carlo and Nancy, where he became known to the other troops and citizens. It

SERGEANT STUBBY WITH REAL "DOG" TAGS.

Armed Forces History: Smithsonian Institution

was reported that when in Paris with his owner, Stubby saved a young girl from being hit by a car. She had been petting him and started to step in front of a vehicle when our hero pulled her back. Stubby was becoming a legend.

One of his most important accomplishments was to lift morale among the soldiers in what was a hard fought, depressing war. By the end of the war on November 11, 1918 over 9 million people had been killed. Many men perished from disease. The trench warfare, set in a horrific cratered desolate landscape of exploding mines, smoke, and barbed-wire, shattered the nerves of many men. It is remarkable that a little dog stayed with his fellow soldiers, helped lift their spirits and gave them hope of better times to come. Stubby's courage under fire, his stamina and an occasional canine salute, were a delight and morale booster to the fighting men and officers alike.

While in Paris after the Armistice, Stubby was a hit as he met English, Australian, French, and American soldiers. While in Mandres-en-Basigny, France on Christmas Day, 1918, he was greeted by and then offered his paw to President Woodrow Wilson. The President had traveled to France to congratulate and review the victorious troops. After that, Stubby returned to America the way he came, smuggled on board the ship back home. The "tramp dog" (as one article later referred to him) had started out as a volunteer regiment mascot and in true military fashion moved up through the ranks. Private Stubby had been promoted to sergeant, and by the end of the war he was known to every Division and was the mascot of the entire American Expeditionary Force.

After the war, Stubby traveled to different cities throughout the United States. He would sometimes lead or march alongside with the soldiers in veterans' parades. He even flirted with show business and had a few vaudeville performances alongside famous stars, such as legendary actress Mary Pickford. He was world famous and during his life met many dignitaries including Presidents Calvin Coolidge and Warren Harding. General 'Blackjack' Pershing himself, Commander of the A.E.F. during the War, awarded Stubby a Gold Medal from the Humane Education Society for his heroic service and many achievements. He commented that Stubby was "A hero of the highest caliber."

Stubby was honored as a lifetime member of the American Legion, YMCA, and the American Red Cross, for whom he helped recruit members and sell victory bonds. His YMCA membership referred to him as Mr. Stubby and entitled him to "Three Bones a Day" and a place to sleep for life. One of his proudest moments was at the exclusive Boston Dog Show where our rough and tumble street dog was awarded a gold "Hero Dog" medal.

His career was not yet over. In 1921 his owner entered Georgetown University to study law, and his buddy, Stubby, soon became the beloved mascot of the Hoya's football team. He performed lovable antics, including pushing around a football on the field at halftime, to the delight of the crowd. Some people actually believe that this was the beginning of the half-time football game show. What a dog.

In 1922 the newspapers announced that Stubby was given a room at the swanky Hotel Majestic. They lifted their strict ban on dogs to accommodate the famous war hero. He was not only admitted but was given the best room available and a special chef was assigned to his "gustatory" wishes.

Through thick and thin Stubby stayed loyal to his master, J Robert Conroy. He died of old age in Conroy's arms on March 16, 1926. He received a lengthy obituary in the New York Times worthy of his achievements and fame. His body was preserved and for many years he was on display at the Red Cross Museum. After the war he was the subject of many newspaper articles and magazine profiles.

Someone should feature his story in a movie and if they do, I hope that instead of some blow-dried Hollywood purebred they get a tough little mixed breed bull dog to play Stubby. I think his old comrades would appreciate that.

In 1978 a children's book was published "Stubby-Brave Soldier

STUBBY GETS AWARD FROM GENERAL PERSHING

Armed Forces History: Smithsonian Institution

Armed Forces History: Smithsonian Institution

YMCA LIFETIME MEMBERSHIP CARD

Armed Forces History: Smithsonian Institution

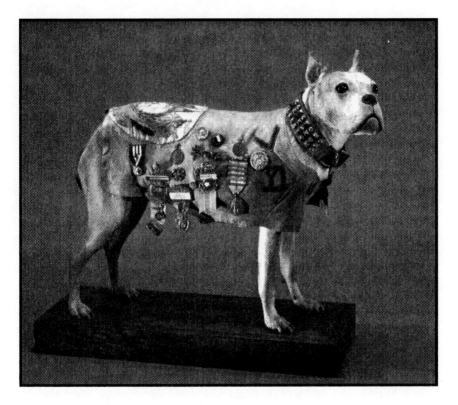

On display at Museum

Armed Forces History: Smithsonian Institution

Sergeant Stubby's Brick at Liberty Memorial

Dog." His fascinating story is being learned by a new generation and his fame seems to be growing. Sergeant Stubby was recently honored, on November 11, 2006, Armistice Day, at the Walk of Honor at the United States World War I Monument in Kansas City, with his own engraved brick.

Stubby still "lives" on, preserved at the Smithsonian Institute in Washington, DC. He stands proudly on display, front and center in "The Price of Freedom: Americans at War" exhibit that opened in 2004. He is adorned to this day wearing his collar and jacket with his many awards attached. In 2012 he was featured, and his story told, on a popular television show "Mysteries at the Museum."

Sergeant Stubby stands as a testament to the power of a little dog to enrich lives and to make our most difficult challenges tolerable.

~

Many dogs were used in World War I, mostly to help search for wounded men. They were also utilized as messengers, and even to deliver food. Unfortunately, from 1914–1918, more than 7,000 dogs were killed in action. Stubby had indeed been fortunate. After the war it was decided to build a monument to these loyal dogs.

At Hartsdale Pet Cemetery in New York there now stands a beautiful bronze statue of a Shepherd dog wearing a Red Cross blanket. He stands alertly atop an imposing tall granite base. At the dog's feet are a bronze helmet and canteen. A ceremony is held at the site every year on Memorial Day. There is a nice inscription on the monument which reads as follows;

Dedicated to the Memory of the War Dog
Erected By Public Contributions By Dog Lovers
To Man's Faithful Friend for the Valiant Services Rendered
in the Warld War 1914-1918

WAR DOG MEMORIAL AT HARTSDALE CEMETERY

CHAPTER 4

RIN TIN TIN

There will always be a Rin Tin Tin

—Lee Duncan

I am constantly amazed at how anytime and anywhere a few simple events can change history and the course of our lives forever. According to the owner of world famous Rin Tin Tin, one such occasion was September 15, 1918 on a battlefield in Lorraine, France.

World War I was drawing to a close. An American soldier, Corporal Leland Duncan, was fighting in France as a gunner with the 135th Aero Squadron. One fortunate day he happened to check out a recently bombed dog kennel and found a shell shocked dog with her newly born pups. He rescued and adopted two of the pups and named them in honor of popular small yarn dolls given by the locals to soldiers for good luck; Rintintin and Nannette.

He nursed the newborn pups with whatever resources he could find and kept them alive despite the difficult circumstances of the battlefield. Before the war ended Duncan was wounded in action

DUNCAN & RINTINTIN IN FRANCE 1918

Courtesy: Riverside Metropolitan Museum

YOUNG RINTY CLIMBING 11 FEET, 9 INCHES!

Courtesy: Riverside Metropolitan Museum

and received several medals, including what is now called the Purple Heart. One of the pups he found, Rin Tin Tin, would go on to become world famous and one of the biggest movie stars Hollywood ever produced.

As Lee told the story, before he left France, he visited with the captured German Kennel Master who had known the dogs before the bombing. From their conversations he had a chance to find out more about the pups. They were out of 'Betty des Flandres', and sired by 'Fritz de la Chasse Royale', two registered quality pedigree dogs of the fairly new German Shepherd breed. The pups' lineage was later traced back to 1899 and Horand, who was the first registered German Shepherd dog. Luckily, Duncan was able to get permission to bring the dogs on the long return voyage home. Unfortunately, Nanette became ill and died shortly after reaching the United States.

After their arrival back in the United States, Duncan and Rin Tin Tin went on to their home in Los Angeles, California. Lee returned to his job as a salesman at a large sporting goods store, where he met and became friends with many people who would help him later with his Hollywood aspirations.

When he wasn't busy at work, Lee spent countless hours training Rin Tin Tin, who proved to be an able student and great companion. Rinty, as he was nicknamed by his owner, had extraordinary athletic ability and could leap long distances and climb incredible heights. Most of the training was aimed at war and police work. Over the next few years he would regularly exhibit and enter Rinty in various dog shows and competitions in the Los Angeles area.

At some point it occurred to Duncan that his dog was special and had the intelligence and talent to perform in motion pictures. Dogs had played an important role from the earliest days of cinema. Since the movies were silent, a dog was not at much disadvantage over two legged actors. People craved action with a strong dose of emotion, and dogs gave them all that and more. One early canine star was a dog named "Rover," whose fame resulted in his name becoming one of the most popular ever for a dog. Another Shepherd dog named Strongheart was well known in movies and Duncan was sure his dog was better. He later wrote "I was so excited over the motion picture idea that I found myself thinking about it night and day."

A combination of trends all aligned to help fulfill Duncan's dream. During the 20's the German Shepherd breed would rise from obscurity and became America's dog of choice. Instead of short films, audiences were demanding feature length movies, especially those that highlighted old fashioned family values. Movies that catered to children and young people were drawing the largest audiences. It was the perfect storm for the home spun action adventure films that dogs starred in.

Duncan trudged across Hollywood looking for his big breakthrough. Eventually he was at the right place at the right time. Persistence and opportunity finally met and Rinty stepped in and played a bit part as a wolf in "The Man from Hell's River" (1922). His ability to perform caught the eye of Harry Warner, one of the owners of the fledgling Warner Brothers Studio. Lee had a script he had written, and soon Rin Tin Tin had his first starring role in a hugely successful picture, "Where the North Begins" (1923). A star was born. He would eventually go on to perform in at least 26 films over the next decade. During that time movie attendance grew quickly and the demand for action pictures with a sound moral message ensured that the movies Rinty starred in were well attended. The huge success of Rin Tin Tin's movies is credited with saving the fledgling Warner Brothers Studio from bankruptcy several times over his career.

Most of the films Rin Tin Tin starred in were silent melodramas. He and his Hollywood contemporary Shepherd rivals, Braveheart and Peter the Great, were often type cast and portrayed as either half-wolf, or shown reverting to the feral state from which they had supposedly come. Most of the settings were westerns and other action genres set outdoors. Film critics of the day praised Rinty and his acting talent. He often stole the show and made an otherwise forgettable movie

PLAYING LEAPFROG WITH HOLLYWOOD FRIENDS

Courtesy: Riverside Metropolitan Museum

PUBLICITY PHOTO

www.RinTinTin.com

entertaining. One critic noted that the "human acting is subordinate to that of the dog." Others noted that children (and their parents) were mesmerized by the dog's ability to elicit sympathy and portray affection, rage and cunning. In scenes that "seemed like asking almost too much of any animal," Rinty dazzled the critics, and terms such as "remarkable performance" and "consistently amazing" peppered their reviews.

At the end of his breakthrough movie, "Where the North Begins," we see Rin Tin Tin with one of his costars, Nanette. She was a pedigreed Shepherd also owned by Frank Duncan. The final scene of the movie has Rinty and Nanette showing off their pups for an audience pleasing happy ending. The pups were really theirs. Nanette appeared in a few movies but was mostly used for breeding, advertising and publicity. Part of Rin Tin Tin's success was his image as a hard working actor who went home to his "wife" and pups after a hard day's work. The studio and his owner worked hard to portray him as a wholesome family 'man' with carefully crafted publicity campaigns. People and children enjoyed the charade and Rinty's popularity soared.

Unlike some actors, Rinty did make the successful transition later in his career to talking or more fittingly 'barking' pictures. Unfortunately the majority of the films he made, including some of his best, have been lost, and only a handful remain. Although a star, Rinty usually performed most of his own fantastic stunts. He possessed a dog's natural athletic ability and raised the exploits of dogs in show business to new levels. One unique quality that set him apart from other movie mutts was his seemingly genuine ability to act. He stood out by being able to convey courage, intelligence and emotion to his movie audience.

Rin Tin Tin became a household name and a national sensation. He went Hollywood! Thousands of fan letters poured in every week asking about the dog. Some fans were rewarded with paw print signed photos or were even able to meet the star at public appearances.

CAVORTING WITH CONTEMPORARY MOVIE STARS, JANE WINTON & MYRNA LOY

Courtesy: Riverside Metropolitan Museum

RIN TIN TIN AND NANETTE

Courtesy: Riverside Metropolitan Museum

Interestingly, on one publicity tour to the Portland area he even paid his respects at the grave of Bobbie "The Wonder Dog" (Chapter 7). He was also awarded the ultimate Hollywood tribute with a paw marked cement square on "The Walk of Fame." He was a star with all the trimmings. He even sported a diamond dog collar, rode in a limo and had a personal chef to prepare his steak dinners. And while he stayed in a kennel most of the time, he did eat out of a silver dog dish.

Rin Tin Tin and other canine stars had a large impact on American culture. Over the last century, dogs have made the transition from farm and work animals that mostly lived out in the yard, to the pampered members of the household we see today. Rinty traveled the country, met famous people and made hundreds of personal appearances. He did a lot of public relations work as a Red Cross dog. Over the years Rinty's popularity and endorsements have helped and made many people happy, besides selling a lot of merchandise and dog food.

As implausible as it seems, Rinty also had a career in radio. His radio series in the early 30's was originally called "The Wonder Dog" and eventually it was changed to "Rin Tin Tin." After his death Rin Tin Tin Jr. took over the role.

Rin Tin Tin died in August 1932. According to Hollywood legend he died in the arms of actress Jean Harlow who lived across the street. There was a public outpouring of grief for the dog and his unexpected death. Although originally buried at home it was decided to return him to his native country France for permanent burial.

On the banks of the Seine River just outside Paris is a special cemetery reserved for animals only. Cimetiere des Chiens was founded in 1899 in response to recently passed strict laws regarding disposal of dead animals. Today the cemetery hosts thousands of animal graves, mostly cats and dogs, but also including a monkey, a rabbit, a sheep, several horses and even a lion. It is dominated by a large monument dedicated to Barry, the great Saint Bernard (Chapter 2). There is also a shelter for the local (live) cats, who roam freely around the grounds. But the most famous inhabitant is Rin Tin Tin whose monument

Courtesy: Riverside Metropolitan Museum

RINTY & JUNIOR SELLING DOG FOOD

Courtesy: Riverside Metropolitan Museum

"Life's 'little' Troubles"
Rin-Tin-Tin   Nannette

DINNER WITH THE FAMILY AT THE TABLE

Courtesy: Riverside Metropolitan Museum

HELPING ORPHANAGE

Courtesy: Riverside Metropolitan Museum

RINTY GOES FOR A SCOOT!

Bubba visiting RinTinTin Hollywood Star on Walk of Fame.

www.RinTinTin.com

is still frequently visited. He was born September 10, 1918 and died August 10, 1932. This is the inscription on his monument:

Rin Tin Tin
La Grande Vedette
Du Cinema

After his death and even to this day, the name lives on. The original Rinty sired many pups and one was chosen as Rin Tin Tin Jr. Some of the other pups found homes with famous stars including Greta Garbo and Jean Harlow. Junior carried on the name and even teamed up with Rex "The Wild Horse" for a few films. While not as prolific as his father, Junior appeared in at least 12 movies between 1932 and 1939.

The star of the next generation was Rin Tin Tin III, who only made a couple of films. But while not achieving the cinematic success of his father and grandfather he was successful in other ways. Duncan and Rin Tin Tin III helped train over 5,000 dogs for the U.S. Military K9 Corp for service in World War II. A very important role that would have made his grandfather proud.

Rin Tin Tin IV is the dog that was probably the best known to my generation. He starred in the very popular 1950's television series "The Adventures of Rin Tin Tin." Although four dogs were used for the filming, Rin Tin Tin IV was the lead dog for the series. The show ran from October 1954 until May 1959, and was set at a U.S. Cavalry frontier post, (Fort Apache) in the 1870's. Every week Rinty fought the bad guys, saved lives and came to the rescue, much to the early television audience's delight. The show and dogs popularity gave rise to a marketing tidal wave of memorabilia, books, and toys. Rinty was once again a household name and a Hollywood star to a new generation of fans.

After Lee Duncan's death in 1960, the bloodline continued in Texas. Jannettia Brodsgaard Propps had known Mr. Duncan and

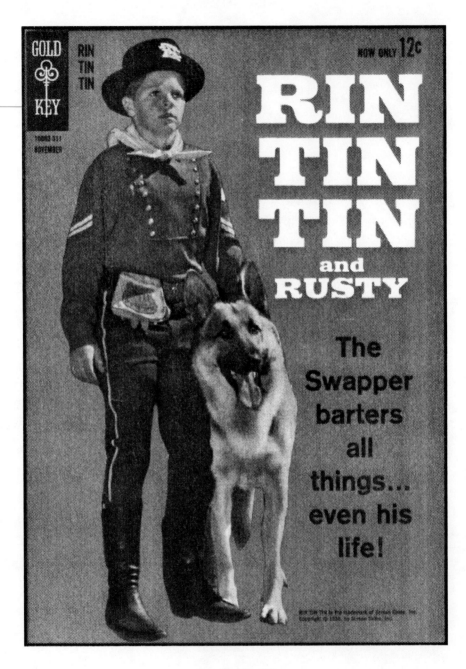

RinTinTin IV

acquired four of Rin Tin Tin's pups during the years before he died. With Lee's help and blessings she managed the careful breeding of successive Rintys. Her granddaughter, Miss Daphne Hereford assisted her and took over the program in 1988. Currently Mrs. Propps' great-granddaughter Dorothy Yanchak is in charge of the ongoing top quality breeding program.

They continue to produce award winning dogs that Lee and Rinty would be proud of. Their dedication to the lineage has consistently produced dogs who have won many awards including multiple American Kennel Club Companion titles. It remains one of the oldest continuous bloodlines in the breeds' history. Many of the authentic Rin Tin Tin dogs they produce are also trained as service dogs for special needs children. The latest namesake of Rinty is RinTin Tin XII, who carries on the name to a new generation of fans. True to the breed, he is a beautiful, intelligent dog, sable grey in color. Rin Tin Tin lives on and still makes appearances at special events across the country.

It just goes to show that you never know how a little bundle of fur is going to change your life. So be nice to your dog. You might just end up riding in a limousine next to a diamond studded canine super star. GO RINTY!!!

A New Generation; Jannettia Brodsgaard Propps with Rintys' Progeny

www.RinTinTin.com

RIN TIN TIN GRAVESITE – PET CEMETERY NEAR PARIS

www.RinTinTin.com

CHAPTER 5

DOG ON THE TUCKERBOX

Dogs wait for us faithfully
—Marcus Tillius Cicero

For our next canine story we journey 'Down Under' to the continent of Australia. This dog born of legend has no name but is a famous part of the Aussie folklore, identity and pride. About half way between Sydney and Melbourne at Snake Gully, five miles north of Gundagai, New South Wales, is located the 'Dog on the Tuckerbox' historical monument. It has become an icon to the past. Inspired by a poem, the monument pays homage to the loyal dogs that accompanied the hard driving bullock drivers who forged their way into Australia's interior frontier in the 19th century.

In the early 1800's explorers and settlers left the coastal areas near the Colonial headquarters in Sydney and crossed the Blue Mountains. These hardy pioneers spread out to the west into the country's wide

EARLY DOG ON TUCKERBOX MONUMENT

BULLOCK TEAM IN OUTBACK

open vast resource rich interior, the 'Outback'. Bullocks became the means to haul supplies and stores, and provide the muscle needed to work and travel the rough terrain in this new and desolate land. It was hazardous country with poorly marked tracks and trails for the bullock teams to negotiate. Sometimes the teams would be stranded for days, bogged down, broken down or stopped by rising water levels at crossings such as Muttama and Adelong Creek.

Oxen, or bullocks as they are referred to in Australia, are usually yoked in pairs. A light load might only require one pair; additional pairs are added as needed for the load being hauled, and a team pulling a heavy load over difficult terrain might have 10 pair or even more. The teams are taught to respond to the signals of the driver or bullocky. Although slower, by use of the yoke, oxen can pull heavier loads for a longer period of time than horses.

The colorful men who became adept at handling these large strong beasts were known as Bullockies, and the drivers were generally referred to as Bullocky Bill. Most drivers were known for their loud voices and forthright language. They were accompanied by their dogs that served as lookouts, helped control the bullocks and of course provided companionship. The hardships and adventures of these men gave inspiration to legend, colorful songs and poems that were spread and recited around the campfires and along the trails. While camped or drinking together they would entertain each other by telling stories, doggerels and rhymes picked up and shared along the way.

One such story outlined the main themes in Bullocky Bill's life, the harsh conditions, his team, his dog and his tuckerbox. A tuckerbox is where the food was stored, a very important item out in the wilderness. If a Bullocky was broke down and stranded alone he would have to go for help and leave the dog behind to guard the team and supplies. A few lines probably originated by one such teamster eventually became the poem that inspired the monument.

The original Dog on the Tuckerbox poem has been attributed to a mysterious Charlie 'Bowyang' Yorke and was first printed in

1857. These men were tough with that adventurous Aussie spirit and sense of humor found among men who work under the harshest conditions. Although there is no definitive copy of the original, here is one version:

As I was coming down Conroy's Gap
I heard a maiden cry;
'There goes Bill the Bullocky,
He's bound for Gundagai.
A better poor old bugger
Never earnt an honest crust,
A better poor old bugger
Never drug a whip through dust.'
His team got bogged at the Nine Mile Creek,
Bill lashed and swore and cried;
'If Nobby don't get me out of this,
I'll tattoo his bloody hide.'
But Nobby strained and broke the yoke,
And poked out the leader's eye;
Then the dog sat on the tucker box
Nine miles from Gundagai.

Another early version:

Good morning mate, you are too late
The shearing is all over,
Tie up your dog behind the log
Come in and have some dover.
For Nobby Jack has broke the yoke,
Poked out the leader's eye
And the dog sat on the tucker box,
Nine miles from Gundagai.

Folklore, poems and subsequent songs paid tribute to Bullocky Bill's dog. He was such a great loyal dog that he guarded over the driver's tuckerbox by sitting on top and guarding it while Bill was away. People like to think the loyal dog was guarding the tuckerbox but others find the poem makes more sense that instead of 'sat', the dog 'shat' upon the tuckerbox as the fitting end to a day where everything goes wrong. A later much different version, which became very popular, was written by Jack Moses and uses some of the same language and the catchy lines about the dog, tuckerbox and Gundagai.

Gundagai, founded in 1828, is located on the banks of the Murrumbidgee River which helped insure its importance as a place of commerce. Jack Moses was a traveling wine salesman who also wrote poetry and loved the Outback. He wrote his version of the poem in the 1880's and that version was published and became very popular. A Street in Gundagai is now named Moses Avenue in his honor.

The popularity of the poem and its reference to Gundagai triggered people coming into the area to look around. To satisfy their curiosity, in 1926 a replica of a dog sitting on a tuckerbox was hoisted up on a tall pole at a location 9 miles from Gundagai. This gave the tourists something to look at, and a place to spend their money.

During the depression the Gundagai District Hospital was in desperate need of money and needed help. To assist in fundraising, the town decided to capitalize on the popularity of the 'Dog on the Tuckerbox" poem and songs. They decided to build a memorial to the pioneers who had helped forge this great country and to give the tourists a more permanent landmark. They commissioned a local artist and stonemason, Frank Rusconi, to bring the dog to life and to design and build the monument.

The life-size statue of the dog was modeled after a local dog and cast in bronze in Sydney; the base was created in marble. A nationwide competition was held for the inscription on the base and Brian Fitzpatrick of Sydney won, with the following;

Courtesy: Gundagai Library

Earth's self upholds this monument
To conquerors who won her when,
Wooing was dangerous, and now
are gathered unto her again.

After considerable discussion the monument was placed at a convenient location a little closer to town, 5 miles from Gundagai instead of the 9 mentioned in the poem.

In 1932, the local 'Back to Gundagai' picnic turned into a special celebration that benefited the hospital and helped put the town on the map. The yearly celebration commemorated the crossing of the river to Gundagai by Australian explorer Captain Charles Sturt in 1829. On November 28th, 1932, before a crowd estimated at 3,000 people, the Prime Minister of Australia, Joseph Lyons, unveiled the monument as a lasting tribute to the early Australian Outback pioneers. The Prime Minister's comments that day included the following; "...today people do not show sufficient self-reliance, and seek too readily the aid of governments, ... let us follow the example of the pioneers, who fought their own difficulties and won through." Well said.

While it remains unknown if the dog was a hero or not and there is still a controversy over exactly what he did to that Tuckerbox, one thing is certain; there were many loyal dogs that stood by their masters as they faced the trials of the bush during those harsh early days in the great soul of Australia, the Outback.

The "Dog on the Tuckerbox" festival has been held every year since 1992 at the site in November.

It all started with a few lines written by a Bullocky about his dog.

You can still visit the Pioneer Monument today, located off the Hume Highway, 386 kilometers from Sydney, and see for yourself the Dog on the Tuckerbox.

History of the 5 Mile Gundagai

"Earth's self upholds this monument
To conquerors who won her when
Wooing was dangerous, and now
Are gathered unto her again."

This Monument is the gift of the Citizens of Gundagai, and is a tribute to the pioneers of Australia. The spot on which it stands was the famous camping ground of the bullockies, teamsters, and settlers who followed close on the heels of Hume and Hovell from 1824. These hardy sons of Australia facing the unknown, struck this Hume Highway with their caravans whilst passing on to the present great Riverina.

In later years the discovery of gold in this district brought a rush of many thousands, and this spot, with its Hotel, the ruins of which can still be seen at back of Monument and its racecourse, became the rendezvous of all classes, including bushrangers, some of whom danced at the Hotel and raced their horses at the race meetings.

It was whilst escorting gold along this road that Sergeant Parry, of Gundagai, was shot dead by Gilbert, of Ben Hall's gang. Later "Moonlight" and his gang also exploited this territory and were afterwards captured and tried at the present Gundagai Court-house for the murder of Senior Constable Bowen, whose remains, together with those of two of the bushrangers—Nesbitt and Wrenecke—rest in the Gundagai Cemetery.

This Card Bears a Royalty of 2d. to the Gundagai District Hospital.

Courtesy: Gundagai Library

Dog on the Tuckerbox.
Unveiling Ceremony.

MONUMENT UNVEILED IN 1932

Courtesy: Gundagai Library

CHAPTER 6

HACHI-KO

The eyes reveal the wisdom of the heart

In the midst of the largest population center in the world, a lone dog sits waiting for his master to come home. The master will never return, and a life sized bronze statue has now replaced the living dog, standing as a monument to Hachiko's 10 year vigil.

Approximately 35 million people live in and around the amazing city of Tokyo, Japan. At the Shibuya railroad station, a famous popular landmark and place to meet, is the statue of Hachiko, Japan's most faithful and famous dog. His undying loyalty and devotion to his master touched the heart of the people who inhabit this island nation. A country's heroes are a reflection of the values the culture holds in highest regard. In Japan, loyalty is one of those values.

Hachiko was one of Japan's own breed of dog, the Akita, originally known as the Odate dog. The ancestors of today's dog can be seen carved on the artifacts of ancient Japanese archeology. They are known as fierce and courageous watchdogs and hunting dogs. Yet they make

HACHIKO WITH COLLAR

great pets, and are good natured and docile loyal companions. They had been bred by, and to have the qualities of, a Samurai–brave, strong, and loyal to death. It is said that Japanese mothers would routinely leave their children under the protective watch of the trustworthy family Akita dog.

Japan's borders were closed to most foreigners for hundreds of years before the historic arrival of Commodore Mathew Perry from the United States in 1853. To help celebrate his arrival and as tokens of friendship he brought gifts for the Emperor, Empress and other important Japanese officials. Perry's goal was to establish relations and open up Japan as a trading partner. The items he presented were meant to demonstrate the many goods that the United States had to offer. He presented a variety of interesting things including a complete telegraph set, books and survey charts, maps, perfumes, clocks, champagne, whiskey and even a telescope. He also brought one gift that would resonate with the Japanese and forever change their lives. It was a ¼ size, scaled-down railroad system, including the locomotive, railroad cars and even the track. Given as an example of western technology, it was setup and demonstrated. The Japanese loved it. People lined up to take turns riding around sitting on the cars. Trains became very popular, a symbol of the progress and modernization of Japan, and eventually the predominant mode of transportation. Trains and train stations would play a big part in the life of Hachi.

In the following years, trade and interaction with the west flourished. Besides introducing new goods and ideas the foreigners also brought different varieties of dogs to the islands. Of course, some of these dogs interbred with the local dogs. This caused some concern and there was a renewed interest in the history of and preservation of purely Japanese dogs. In an effort to preserve the Odate breed, the Akita-inu Preservation Society was formed. Efforts were made to recognize and standardize the dogs and to develop a true breed. It was eventually decided to call the breed, Akita.

SHIBUYA STATION–PREWAR

Hidesaburo Ueno was a professor at the University of Tokyo. The era of nationalism had inspired educated people like him to search for and acquire distinctively Japanese dogs for their pets. One of his former students and friends helped him find just what he was looking for. In November, 1923, a new litter had been born on a farm near Odate in Akita Prefecture. These were the native dogs the professor had been looking for. The arrangements were made and the puppy was acquired and transported by train to Tokyo. It was a long train ride and the puppy, that had been sent in a sack, almost died on the long trip. The professor's gardener, Kikusaburo 'Kiku' Kobayashi picked up the pup at the train station and took him home. He was named Hachi-ko because he was the eighth dog that the family had raised. Hachi means eight and 'ko' is a term of endearment. The symbol for eight also symbolizes success and prosperity in Japan.

Hachi had moved into a very nice home, the largest and finest in the neighborhood. The professor taught agriculture and was highly respected in his field. He was dedicated to Japan becoming self-sufficient by more efficient agricultural techniques. The small island country had to rely on imported food to survive. He was highly renowned in his field and had even been invited to receive a Medal of Honor award at the Emperor's New Year banquet.

Hachi lived like a prince. When he was old enough he would go out on walks with his master. Every morning the professor would walk to the train station and head off to his job at the University. In the evening Mr. Ueno would be greeted by his waiting dog when he stepped off the train.

One fateful day in May 1925, the professor did not return. He had taken ill and died at work. Hachi waited and waited. Every day Hachi would watch the trains arrive and hope for his master to return. People tried to adopt him and took him home, but he would always escape and return to wait. A friend of the professor would take him food. He was also fed and given attention by kindhearted train station commuters who understood what had happened and why he waited. They were sad because they knew that the master he waited for would never return. The story circulated and sympathetic people would pet, feed and even pray for him.

Eventually the professors old friend Kiku, accepted responsibility and provided care for the dog. Since he lived close to the station Hachi could continue his daily trip to wait for the evening train. Sadly, it was not too long before Kiku himself passed away. After his death, Hachi wandered the streets, staying close to the Shibuya station and his daily vigil. Vendors and shopkeepers in the area began to know him and would occasionally give him something to eat. It was reported that he had a special fondness for Yakitori.

Hachiko's daily routine was to go to the train station every day and wait for the evening train to come in. He would lay there and scan the departing passengers looking for his owner. The conductors, ticket agents and others at the station soon became his friends. The stationmaster especially grew fond of Hachi and set aside a small storeroom for him to sleep in. When not watching for his master's return he survived by living as a street dog.

In October 1932, the nation's largest newspaper ran an article that would cause a sensation and put Hachi in the national spotlight. It was titled, "A Moving Story of an Old Dog." The story made him a celebrity and he became the talk of Tokyo. It also created a new awareness and pride in the Akita breed. Crowds of Tokyoites would gather at the station to witness for themselves the loyal Samurai dog.

In Japan's earlier feudal society a Samurai was a highly trained warrior who was strictly loyal and fought for his lord. When a Samurai's lord was defeated and killed in battle, he was set loose to wander on his own. He was now Ronin. A Ronin was self-reliant and lived by the code of Bushido, still loyal to his deceased lord. That is how the country saw Hachi. Despite the opportunities to live a life with another master Hachi chose to wander the streets, fend for himself, and remained a proud wanderer, forever loyal to his master.

Inspired by the story and the public recognition of the dog's

OUT IN PUBLIC

ON THE STREETS

HACHIKO'S GRAVE IN AOYAMA CEMETERY, MINATOKU, TOKYO, JAPAN

Photo Credit: Hakaishi

loyalty it was decided by citizens of Tokyo to erect a statue in the dog's honor. A design was proposed and an artist was commissioned for the project. Hachiko was taken several times to the artist's studio to pose for the project.

1934 was known as the Year of The Dog. In April of that year, a celebration was organized to honor Hachi and to unveil the life sized statue. Not many legends are still alive when their monuments are erected. Hachi was washed up for the special occasion, given a nice new collar, and was adorned with a large ribbon to wear. More than 3,000 people crowded into Shibuya Station to applaud and witness the unveiling. They say every dog has his day and Hachiko had his. The aging loyal dog's vigil would continue almost another year until his death on March 8, 1935. He had become so famous that there was a national day of mourning for the dog.

Helen Keller visited Japan in 1937. She had heard about Hachi and was interested in his story. She was so impressed that she acquired an Akita dog, which helped to give the breed international attention. Despite their designation as a national monument in 1931, barely a dozen dogs of the breed survived the disasters of World War II. Their popularity resurged after the war. The breeding programs resumed and in the following years many were taken back to the United States by the occupying soldiers. The large strong dogs love snow and cold weather. The pure strain of Akita was proudly used as sled dogs for Japanese Antarctic expeditions. Today there are many regional and color variations but strict guidelines, including the upright ears and curled tail, still identify this large dog breed.

In 1944 the original Hachi statue was melted down for war material. Another statue that had been placed at the Odate train station in 1935 was also destroyed. The statue we see today was erected in 1948. It was cast by Takeshi Ando, son of the original artist, Sho Ando. The statue in Odate was replaced in 1987. In 2004 another statue was erected in front of the Akita Dog Museum in Odate. The station stop at Shibuya is now named "Hachiko-Guchi," Hachiko Exit. Hachi has

MONUMENT AND STATUE AT SHIBUYA STATION, TOKYO, 2011

Photo Credit: Gail Sumpter

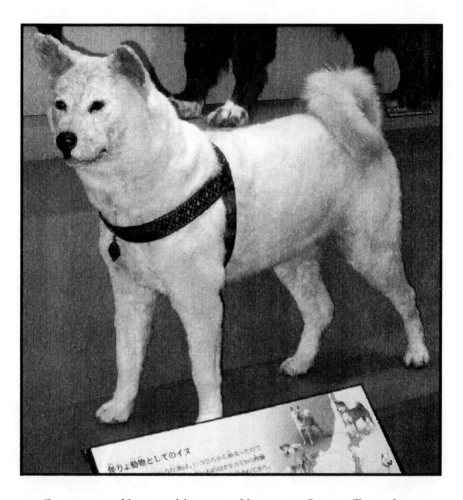

ON DISPLAY AT NATIONAL MUSEUM OF NATURE AND SCIENCE, TOKYO, JAPAN

Photo Credit: Muramasa, Muramasa

been the subject of many movies and books.

Every year on April 8th the dog is honored at a ceremony of remembrance at the crowded and busy Shibuya railroad station. One ceremony witnessed by hundreds of people was described as follows: A lei of fresh flowers was put on Hachiko's statue, which had been surrounded by the fruits, vegetables, and ceremonial bottles of sake demanded by Shinto ritual. The silk robed Shinto priests in tall lacquered black hats, solemnly read eulogies to Hachiko in classical Japanese from old fashioned rice paper scrolls. They wave green branches of the sakaki tree, a type of laurel, to purify the air. They then bow to the statue, followed by each priest clapping his hands twice, to summon the attention of the spirits. It is clear that the legendary dog's place is secure as a national treasure and in the hearts of the Japanese people.

He lives on in his monuments and his body is preserved at the National Science Museum in Tokyo where he can be seen today. He is loved for his spirit of family loyalty that all should hope to achieve. He had only lived with his master a year and a half yet his loyalty never ceased. No matter what, he went on despite the hardships life threw at him. His bones were eventually buried in the cemetery next to his master, Professor Ueno. He is known in Japan as Chuken (faithful dog) Hachiko and he continues to warm the hearts of those who hear his story today.

CHAPTER 7

BOBBIE
THE WONDER DOG

*...the most extraordinary achievement of intelligence
and loyalty ever recorded to the glory of dogdom...*

—Frank Brazier

Of all the dog stories I have heard this is the one that is absolutely the most amazing. It seems hard to believe, but a family goes on vacation, loses their family dog over 2,500 miles from home and lo and behold, six months later the dog finds his way back and shows up at their doorstep. He was known as Bob, Bobbie, and "Silverton Bobbie" or more appropriately "Bobbie the Wonder Dog" and his true story inspired books, movies and was a national sensation.

Silverton is located in the Willamette Valley east of Salem in Oregon. This fertile valley was one of the final destinations for thousands of travelers who made the long journey from St Louis in the 1800's, on the historic Oregon Trail.

Our hero is a Scotch Collie also known as a Farm Collie. These

Courtesy: Silverton Country Historical Society

beautiful large dogs are known for their obedience, agility and ability to herd livestock. They also seem to have the innate desire and ability to find their way back to home and master. One of the most popular breeds at the turn of the 20th century, their number has dwindled as the population has migrated from farms to more urban living.

In 1919, Elizabeth and Frank Brazier purchased a farm and moved to Silverton, Oregon. Soon thereafter they acquired a naturally bobtailed Scotch Collie pup they named Bobbie. They called him Bob for short and he was there to help out with the livestock and for family companionship. He was a "rollicking, full-of-fun puppy," according to Mr. Brazier. He was also a very intelligent dog who soon learned to help using his talent for herding animals. He was a natural "heeler." They soon sold the property to a friend and left Bobbie with the new owner. They loved him but thought he would be useful and happier staying on the farm in the country. The Brazier family then purchased a small restaurant (The Reo Cafe) and moved the family into the town, Silverton. After they left him behind, Bobbie would walk into town and searched them out. He was taken back to the farm but kept coming back to see them. Finally, the Braziers bought him back and Bobbie happily moved into town permanently with his family where he belonged.

In August of 1923 the family including the two daughters, Nova and Leona, made a long trip in their automobile, an Overland Red Bird Touring car. They decided to take along the family dog, Bobbie. They travelled across the country east to Wolcott, Indiana to visit friends and family. This was a journey of over 2,500 miles. While on the visit Frank took Bob into town with him to 'tank up' the car. While Frank was busy, Bob was chased by some local dogs and ran off. Frank drove around town the rest of the day honking his horn and searching but to no avail. The family spread the word about their lost dog, continued to search and ran ads in the local paper hoping to find him. After waiting and searching for weeks the brokenhearted

Ready for adventure

Oregon Historical Society bb009627

family reluctantly headed toward home.

Meanwhile Bobbie realized he also wanted to get back to home. No one knows for sure exactly how he did it but apparently he was able to pretty much follow the same route the family had used. Six months later on February 15, 1924, Bobbie came home. Bobbie made it to town and spotted Nova; his journey was over. Nova could barely believe it. The dog flew at her making sobbing sounds while he covered her with kisses. She took him home for an ecstatic family reunion. Bob went rushing through the house looking for Frank. He was asleep upstairs when the family and the dog burst in and woke him up. He thought he must be dreaming as a dirty tongue lapped feverishly at his face and dirty paws jumped up to greet him. The dog was so happy he whined and made sounds of joy. The tired and worn out dog was fed the best food in the house, a thick sirloin steak and a bowl of cream. Bob then collapsed and slept for 3 days, safely back in his old bed.

A veterinarian was called and tended to the injuries the dog suffered during his grueling experience. Bobbie had sore feet, a matted coat and toenails worn down to nothing. He had traveled across the country, and over the formidable Rocky Mountains in the midst of a hard winter. How had he done it? Was it really true? The local paper, The Silverton Appeal ran an article the next week. As the news spread across the country of this truly incredible journey, people who had seen him along the way came forward and pieces of the puzzle started to fall in place.

Letters poured in and information was gathered. People reported seeing and feeding the lost dog all across the country. They wrote in with their stories of the traveling dog and some even sent pictures. Bobbie would accept their kindness, spend a night or two with them, and then with a sense of purpose, move on and keep going. One family even mentioned a piece of broken rope hanging from his collar. They guessed that someone had tried to keep him and he had worked his way loose to continue his

FRANK BRAZIER AND BOBBIE

Oregon Historical Society bb009626

BOBBIE WITH NOVA

Courtesy: Silverton Country Historical Society

trek. A group of hobos came forward and said Bobbie had spent a night in their camp and that they had shared some food and a campfire with the dog after watching him cross a cold river. A photo surfaced of Bobbie in a dog catcher's cage in Des Moines, Iowa. He had been captured, escaped, and was last seen headed west toward home.

He had traveled and was seen in Illinois, Iowa, Nebraska, Colorado, Wyoming, Idaho and Oregon. The Oregon Humane Society conducted an investigation and concluded the story was indeed true and that Bobby had traveled at least 2,800 miles. He had apparently circled the area for a few weeks before he got headed in the right direction. They were able to reconstruct and map the route he probably traveled. The Guinness Book of World Records also substantiated the information that had been gathered and included Bobby in their famous publication.

The people of Silverton were the pioneers and the descendants of the pioneers who had traveled the Oregon Trail west to their new home. It is estimated that up to half of these travelers never made it to their destination. Bobbie's trek was reminiscent of the journey many of their forbearers had made. These were people who could really appreciate the obstacles this dog had overcome; his perseverance and fortitude had earned their respect. Bobbie was a real wonder dog who made them proud to be Oregonians.

Robert Ripley had cartoons created and spread Bobbie's story in his widely syndicated "Believe It Or Not" cartoon pieces that appeared all over the country and in major foreign cities around the world. The dog's story was now well known and marveled at by millions of people.

He was now an international sensation and celebrity. He starred in and played himself in a silent movie titled "The Call of the West," and his story was the inspiration for the hit film, "Lassie Come Home." He was given medals, keys to the city and even allowed to roam the streets, unleashed, with no worry about the dogcatcher.

NEWSPAPER ACCOUNT OF JOURNEY, 1924

Courtesy: Silverton Country Historical Society

BOBBIE "UNDER ARREST" IN DES MOINES, IOWA

Courtesy: Silverton Country Historical Society

In April, 1924 Bobbie was the honored guest at the Home Beautifying Exposition in Portland which was sponsored by the Portland Realty Board. He was displayed with a special miniature house that was custom built for him. Named "Bobbie's Castle," it featured silk curtains and even a fireplace. Over a hundred thousand people came to pet and see "The Wonder Dog" of Silverton in his new house. He was even presented with an inscribed silver collar and the deed to his 'castle' in a special ceremony. It would remain his doghouse for the rest of his life. He even raised a family in his special home. On April 17, 1925 newspapers announced that the Wonder Dog had fallen in love with Tippy and had now become a father with 16 puppies.

In 1927 Bobbie passed away. He had survived his long journey but it had taken a toll on his health. Happily, his last few years were full of fun and good living enjoyed with the family he loved. He was laid to rest at the Oregon Humane Society grounds in Portland Oregon. His special house is also there on display. He was mourned by many and even Rin Tin Tin, the famous Hollywood dog–actor, came and paid his respects, solemnly laying a wreath at his grave.

The Old–Time Scotch Collie Association is dedicated to restoring what they call the Old–Time Scotch Collie, Bobbie's breed. These are such good dogs that it is great to know people are working hard to preserve them.

When dogs were trained for war service it became apparent that the Collie breed was not cut out for ferocious battle. However they did excel as couriers, using their sense of direction and agility to accomplish their mission. They were exceptional at being able to make their way through the battlefield under the harshest conditions, find headquarters, and deliver the messages. They make loving, loyal pets and efforts are now being made to revive this vanishing breed by people who appreciate the special qualities of these beautiful dogs.

In 1932, a pet parade was organized to help honor Bobbie's memory.

"THREE THOUSAND MILES ALONE, ON FOOT, IS A MERE NOTHING WHEN YOU ARE GOIN
HOME TO THOSE YOU LOVE"
BOBBY RECEIVES A MEDAL FROM THE HUMANE SOCIETY

Courtesy: Silverton Country Historical Society

BOBBIE THE "FAMILY MAN"

SOME OF THE PUPS.

RIN TIN TIN AND FRANK BRAZIER LAYING WREATH ON BOBBIE'S GRAVE.

MONUMENT & BOBBIE'S "CASTLE" AT OREGON HUMANE SOCIETY,
PORTLAND, OREGON, 2012

Photo Credit: Kathrin Sumpter

IN HONOR OF
Bobbie the Wonder Dog
A tribute to the affectionate
loyalty of this great Collie.
In 1923-24, lost, he traveled on paws
over 2,500 miles from Indiana
to his home in Silverton.

Dedicated July 10, 2004

His son, Pal, served as the Grand Marshall. It continues to this day every year in May. The people of Silverton still remember their special dog and the festivities include a Bobbie look-alike contest. There is a colorful mural and a replica doghouse in downtown Silverton that keeps him in the public memory. Bobbie truly earned and deserves the title of "Wonder Dog."

Bobbie's Mural
Located on the South Water Street in Silverton, Oregon is a 70-foot long mural that features Bobbie's story.

The above mural photo and the mural photos on the following two pages:

Bobbie mural photographs by Larry Kassell, courtesy Silverton, Oregon Mural Society;
Lori Webb Muralist. Silverton Mural Society website: www.silvertoner.com/murals

Bobbie's Mural continued from the previous page.

Bobbie's Mural continued from the previous page.

CHAPTER 8

WAGHYA

C'mon Baba, Light My Pyre

So now we travel all the way to exotic India and an ancient fortress, Raigaid Fort. Here we find a great monument built to honor Waghya, India's most famous, and faithful dog. His master, Shivaji, sits on his ornate stone throne nearby, not far from his still loyal friend. It is a gorgeous work of art. The remote location, with its panoramic vistas, surrounding ruins, and dramatic background add to the mystical aura these monuments radiate.

The Fort, which is located in the modern day Raigaid District of Maharashtra, is located a few hundred kilometers southeast of Mumbai. Originally built high in the clouds in the year 1030 atop an imposing vertical rock face, it became known as the 'Gibraltar of the East' to the British. Shivaji seized it in 1656, named it Raigaid (The King's Fort), and made it his capital and seemingly impregnable fortress. Over the years, the Fort proved resistant to countless attacks and a daunting obstacle to enemy invaders. In 1818, after many failed

CHHATRAPATI SHIVAJI MAHARAJ

attempts, the British East India Company finally bombarded it into the ruins we see today. The two famous statues stand over the ruins of the historic fort.

On June 6, 1674, Chhatrapati Shivaji Maharaj was crowned sovereign of what eventually became known as the Maratha Empire covering most of the continent of India. He is remembered as a great leader for his efforts to help bring about 'Hindu Swarajya' (Independence for Hindus) to India. He died in 1680.

The inseparable companion of Shivaji, it is said that when Waghya saw his master's body being consumed on the burning pyre, the devoted dog threw himself upon the flames and gave up his life to be with his master.

Built in 1926, Shivaji's grand memorial stands prominently amidst the ruins. He sits atop a replica of his throne and nearby is the monument to Waghya. The dog's memorial was built in 1936 with a large donation from a member of the Dhangar (shepherds) community; members of that group believe the dog to be next to a god. They are both magnificent statues and many tourists today make the long difficult trek up the long, winding 1,450 steps to the ruins. Once there, they are rewarded by the eagle's eye view of the surrounding mountains and countryside, along with the monuments to the king and his faithful dog. There is much to see among the ruins. The six chambers of the queen's quarters, three watchtowers, and remnants of a marketplace are still in place. Other mysterious chambers, walls and fortifications also remain to be seen.

For some it is a sacred place of pilgrimage representing the prophetic vision of Hindu self-rule.

Lately there has been a coordinated effort by various Indian communities to have the monument removed or destroyed. Some insist that the story is a myth, that the height of the dog's statue diminishes the greatness of Shivaji, and that there is little, if any, record of the event.

So I tell the story even if there is some doubt. I also wondered

SHIVAJI'S RAIGAD FORT

Credit: Swapnaannjames at en.wikipedia (http://en.wikipedia.org)

SHIVAJI'S MONUMENT

about the less than warm and fuzzy demise of our hero. But India is a land of diverse and intriguing culture that is indeed foreign and sometimes shocking to our western sensibilities. Scenes of funeral pyres and burning bodies make us realize that life and death have different connotations to different cultures and religions. True or not, the story touches many and it certainly inspired a great monument to be built in memory to the loyalty of a dog.

The greatness of a nation and its moral progress can be judged
by the way in which its animals are treated
—Mahatma Gandhi

WAGHYA'S MONUMENT

www.raigad-fort.info

CHAPTER 9

BALTO AND TOGO

There's no place like Nome

*L*ocated just 150 miles south of the Arctic Circle, is the old gold rush town of Nome, Alaska. It is one of the most isolated communities on the planet. Even today there are no roads connecting this remote coastal city with the rest of the world. When you live this far north it is not much of an exaggeration to say there are only two seasons, winter, and the Fourth of July. Years ago the inhabitants relied on dog teams and sleds for local transportation and as their only connection to the outside world during the long dark winters. In 1925, a frightening deadly epidemic of diphtheria hit the remote village and heroic dogs and men came to the rescue, this is that story.

In the summer of 1898 gold was discovered near Cape Nome by three men who became known as the "Three Lucky Swedes," Jafet Lindberg, Eric Lindblom, and John Brynteson. By the spring of 1899, the spreading news had sparked a gold rush with thousands of prospectors elbowing in to get a share of the riches. Over 8,000 prospectors came from Dawson alone; the scene of the last strike.

Above: NOME BEACH 1899

Clarence Leroy Andrews Photographic Collection; Clarence Leroy Andrews Photographer
Alaska State Library Historical Collections

Below: DOGSLED DELIVERING MAIL IN ALASKA

National Postal Museum; Curatorial Photographic Collection

Nome was unique because much of the gold was easily available on the surrounding beaches. The resulting chaos, lawlessness and tales of greed have been the subject of many court battles, books, plays and Hollywood movies. These were wild times. The population swelled rapidly to over 20,000 people. By 1900 it was the largest General Delivery location in the U.S. Postal system. Out of the chaos, the town was formed, grew and thrived. At its peak, Nome was the most populous city in Alaska. After a few years, the gold played out and the town settled down to a few thousand hardy souls who stayed on to enjoy the isolation and solitude.

Many of the early adventurers were naively ill equipped for the fierce winter conditions they would face. The prospectors that stuck it out learned how to survive from the local Eskimo and Athabascan natives who had lived in the extremely harsh environment for centuries. The savvy newcomers soon traded their boots and jackets for the much more efficient attire they needed, parkas and mukluks.

With ice and snow on the ground most of the year, sleds pulled by teams of dogs became the preferred mode of transportation. A trip by sled is a "mush" and someone who drives a dogsled is known as a "musher." There were so many dog teams running around the city that for safety a law was enacted that required them to wears bells. Besides transportation, the dogs provided the town with a unique and unusual form of entertainment. When the day was over and the hundreds if not thousands of dogs had been fed, one dog would start to howl and the others would join in until every dog in town was howling in unison and a part of the serenading chorus.

The demand for big strong dogs was so great that dogs had to be imported from anywhere along the west coast of America where they could be bought, traded for, or even stolen. Most of the earlier sled dogs were large breeds that were interbred with the native Malamute dogs to produce big cold resistant animals who were able to work in teams and haul heavy loads under the worst subzero conditions.

One of the newcomers who thrived was a wiry Norwegian

named Leonhard Seppala, who had arrived in 1900. Seppala grew fond of smaller, faster dogs recently brought in from neighboring Siberia where they had proven their worth for generations. The Husky dog had been bred to be able to survive the extreme conditions of the frigid north and to have outstanding endurance and speed on the trail. They were endowed with two coats of fur for warmth and protection from water and snow, a large bushy tail that could help cover their face while they slept, almond shaped eyes that protected them from blinding snow and ice and tough paws to withstand the sharp ice. Their trademark piercing light blue eyes and smaller size was a perfect match for Leonhard Seppala, who was also small and tough with the same unusually colored eyes. Seppala learned how to get the best out of his sled dogs, giving them the special food and care they required. Alone in the wilderness the musher's life depended on the proper attention and treatment of his dogs.

"Sepp" demonstrated the worth of these 'new' Siberian Husky dogs by entering them in local sled races which he soon started to regularly win. Seppala and other mushers used their dogs to deliver mail and haul freight, including people and gold, around the area. Seppala had two lead dogs that would become world famous, Balto and Togo. The lead dog was the most important and had to be an intelligent and confident leader of the team. He set the pace and carried out the musher's commands. A good lead dog was essential, very valuable, and vital to successful sledding. He was able to help find the safest route and was carefully chosen because he could save your life.

Named after a Japanese Admiral, Togo had earned his reputation as a great lead dog. Born in October of 1913, he had been a small sickly pup. It looked like he was destined to be a house dog and his owner did not think much of him, at first. But the pup kept breaking loose from the house and kennel and chasing the teams when they went on runs. Finally, one day as the young dog came running after the team once again, Seppala gave in, stopped and hooked him to the harness with the other dogs and gave him a chance. Togo was a happy dog. To his owner's surprise the young dog showed unusual intelligence and natural ability and quickly worked his way up to the front of the team. Togo was as fast as he was tireless.

Balto was a beautiful dog, mostly black with some white on one leg. The record is unclear but he was probably born in 1919. He had been named after Samual Balto, a well-known Norwegian Sami explorer who had visited Nome with his family. Balto was owned and raised by Seppala but because he was not a thoroughbred Husky his owner did not use him on his teams. But the dog would soon have his chance to prove his owner wrong. Balto was destined to become one of the most famous and praised dogs in the world.

Doctor Curtis Welch was the only physician in town. In fact, he was the only doctor for hundreds of miles. In the winter of 1925 he became very alarmed when the first signs of the dreaded illness Diphtheria showed up in town. The town had always prepared for winter carefully, knowing that ships would not be able to reach port with supplies for many months because of the ice bound Bering Sea. Unfortunately when the last supply ship arrived that season the Diphtheria antitoxin serum that the doctor had ordered did not arrive. He only had a few doses in his possession and those were old and probably unusable.

Years before the small town had suffered from measles and in 1919 influenza had killed a thousand inhabitants, so the news of another epidemic spread fear quickly. These diseases were especially hard on the most vulnerable, the Native Americans and children. The previous 'flu' epidemic had killed half of the native population. Diphtheria is a terrible illness that causes sores in the throat and respiratory system that can lead to a slow strangling of the patient.

Doctor Welch sounded the alarm. He knew he did not have much time to act. Quarantine was declared and public gatherings were forbidden. Welch was the lone doctor in town and he only had a few nurses to help him out. Nurse Emily Morgan was designated to be

BALTO AND GUNNAR

LAPLANDERS (SAMI) BALTO FAMILY ARRIVING IN NOME FROM NORWAY

B.B. Dobbs Photographic Collection: B.B. Dobbs Photographer
Alaska State Library Historical Collections

BALTO AND GUNNAR

Alaska State Library Historical Collections

the quarantine nurse and warning signs started going up at infected homes around town. The doctor quickly sent out an urgent appeal to the outside world in the hopes of finding enough antitoxin serum to save lives before the highly contagious disease spread through the area. Radio and telegraph were the means of communication to the outside world and the plea traveled quickly. Nome's predicament soon made front page headlines in most major U.S. newspapers.

Some supplies of serum were located in Anchorage and there were even more in Seattle. While not enough by itself, if they could get the doses in Anchorage, they could hold out for the few weeks it would take to get the supply in Seattle shipped to Alaska. The big problem was that it was over 1,000 miles from Anchorage to Nome. It seemed to some that the only option at that time of the year was probably by train and dogsled. The first leg of the journey north, from Anchorage to Nenana, was covered by railroad. That could be done in 12 hours. Then the serum would have to move west from Nenana to Nome, which would be a rough 674 mile trip by dog sled. There was an existing trail since the journey was regularly made to get mail through, even in the winter. But the trip regularly took 4 weeks or more, depending on weather. By then the epidemic could sweep through town and take many lives.

Some people argued for an airplane to make the trip. Aviation in Alaska was still in the experimental phase, and was obviously the way of the future, but planes were still open cockpit and navigation equipment could not yet be trusted that close to the North Pole. Being the middle of winter made the trip especially risky due to brutally cold weather and unforeseen storms. A crash would not only harm the pilot but destroy the vaccine. The territorial Governor, Scott Bone weighed the arguments on both sides and made the tough decision to use the more traditional yet slower method of Alaskan transportation, dog sleds.

The news of the pending rescue attempt and the dire situation was carried worldwide. The relatively new era of radio allowed listeners to follow the situation in real time as it occurred. People across the country were transfixed by the unfolding crisis. This was something new. In the preceding few years the number of radios found in United States homes had increased exponentially from a few thousand to over 3 million. People around the world listened live to the daily drama of this real life adventure; the race to save lives in a small remote Alaskan village.

The plan was to use a relay team of 20 mushers and over 150 dogs. Leonhard Seppala and his team lead by his trusted dog Togo, volunteered to help out with the effort. He had an 8 year old daughter at home and was very worried about her. He would take off from Nome with a team of 20 dogs, intercept the relay and help get the serum back in time.

Balto would go with Gunner Kaason, another musher trying to help. Balto was not very experienced but Gunner recognized the intelligence and potential in this strong young dog and felt that he was up to the task. Kaason and Seppala both took off from Nome and would each meet the relay at different points, then turn around and come back.

The serum was rushed to the train and sent the 298 miles to Nenana. On January 27th, it arrived and was transferred to the first dog team. The 20 pounds of vaccine had been wrapped in blankets and padding to cushion and protect it from the cold weather. It was vital that occasionally the bundle was warmed up to prevent freezing which could ruin the serum. By the time the vaccine was transferred to the first dog team the coldest weather in 20 years was starting to set in. The temperature actually dropped to 40 degrees or more below zero for much of the trip.

The first musher took the package and headed out into the cold night. At this time of the year the teams would be making most of the cold difficult trip in darkness. There was only about 4 hours of faint light each day from about 10 until 2. The majority of the relay mushers were Native Americans. Many of them regularly used this

Gunnar Kasson + Balto
in their Race to Nome.

BALTO AND GUNNAR

Alaska State Library Historical Collections

trail hauling freight and as U.S. mail carriers. They knew what was at stake. These volunteers were experienced mushers and knew the route and hazards better than anyone.

All of the dog teams on the relay worked hard and many suffered the consequences of frostbite, worn out dogs and fatigue. They literally risked their lives to get that serum on its way. As the relay went on, the life threatening weather was becoming worse and worse. By the time Seppala got the package the weather was probably 50 below zero with gale force winds, fog and blinding snow. He made the decision to take a shortcut over the hazardous exposed ice of the Norton Sound. Seppala and his dog team were almost stranded on breaking ice but Togo saved the day by swimming with a harness to solid ground and heroically pulling them to safety. A disaster was averted and they were able to continue the trip.

The doctor and people of Nome waited anxiously. The storm seemed impossible to get through. Maybe the terrible blizzard had stopped the relay. New cases of the disease were being reported and without the serum the disease could ravage the small town. But despite the storm, on February 2nd the last relay team driven by Gunner and led by Balto, appeared down the beach and arrived safely in Nome. The journey had been accomplished in only 5 and a half days, or 127.5 hours, under the harshest conditions imaginable. Millions of people who had followed the drama were ecstatic; they received a storybook ending to a real life crisis.

The nearly frozen serum was quickly given to the doctor and carefully warmed up. There was worry about whether the serum had been ruined by the freezing temperatures. It was put to use immediately and proved effective. On February 21 the quarantine was lifted and life in Nome returned to normal.

Gunner Kaason and Balto were instantly world famous celebrities. Balto was proclaimed the canine hero by the press. He was a very photogenic and friendly dog, perfect for the role. Modern science had created the serum but it took the old fashioned reliable dogsled to get it through. All of the mushers were proclaimed heroes and each received a gold medal, a reward and a citation for their courageous efforts. Another proud moment was when they were congratulated by the President, Calvin Coolidge.

On the floor of the Senate, the rescue effort was lauded by Senator Dill of Washington State. In praise of Balto he remarked, "This black Siberian dog, through the darkness and storm, crossed this icy desert and kept the trail when no human being could possibly find the way." He went on to remark, "The classic victory of these dogs and men will probably be the last of its kind and is certainly a fitting finish to a long history of brilliant achievement made by dog teams in the Far North." Senator Dill also wanted to make sure and honor the "…unknown Indians and mongrel dog teams used in making some of the most difficult relays of the race against death." He reminded the Senate that the Indians had volunteered for the difficult relays because people in that part of Alaska had been stricken with this dreadful disease over and over again. He wanted the government to take steps to ensure that isolated towns such as Nome received adequate supplies of fresh antitoxin in the future.

Despite some misgivings about Balto receiving so much of the recognition, he had indeed performed heroically under the very worst blizzard conditions. The last leg took them 55 miles into town. The wind turned over the sled several times and Kaason was virtually blinded by the whiteout conditions. At one terrifying moment during the mush, Gunner looked down and saw the serum had fallen off the sled. Luckily he was able to retrace his trail and miraculously he found the bundle before it froze. Gunner always said that Balto had saved his life on the run; he never quit and stayed on the trail despite the blizzard. "It was Balto who led the way, the credit is his."

Gunnar and Balto with the other dogs of his team received and accepted an offer from a Hollywood producer to star in a movie. They soon set off for Washington State and the Mount Rainier area where "Balto's Race to Nome" was filmed. Sadly, no known copies of that film exist today. Gunner and his entire team then set out on a publicity tour that took them on the vaudeville circuit around the United States. Large crowds greeted the celebrities everywhere they traveled. In Hollywood the Mayor of Los Angeles presented Balto with the key to the city.

Within a year after the run, a larger than life bronze statue had been sculpted and erected in New York's Central Park. Balto himself was present for the unveiling on December 17, 1925. The monument stands today as a tribute to the 'serum run' dogs, and as a reminder of the fading Alaskan dog culture. It is larger than life and the back of the dog is kept shiny by the children and tourists who climb up to sit on the bronze statue. The inscription on the plaque reads;

Dedicated to the indomitable spirit of the sled dogs
that relayed antitoxin six hundred miles over rough ice, across
treacherous waters, through Arctic blizzards
from Nenana to the relief of stricken Nome
in the Winter of 1925.
Endurance. Fidelity. Intelligence

After the unveiling, Gunnar, Balto and the rest of his dogs continued their tour of the U.S. Then it all came to a halt. Because of a financial dispute Balto and the team were left behind in Los Angeles and Gunnar Kaason returned to Alaska. The dogs were mistreated and soon started to decline in the warm weather and their new unfamiliar surroundings. In 1927, an ex-boxer from Cleveland named George Kimball heard about and saw for himself their plight, and offered to purchase the dogs. They could be bought for 2,000 dollars. The people of Cleveland collected the money in just 10 days, bought the dogs and rescued them from Los Angeles.

On March 19, 1927, the dogs enjoyed a hero's welcome as they were paraded through downtown Cleveland to the delight of the

KASSON & BALTO AT MONUMENT IN CENTRAL PARK, NEW YORK

Brown Brothers

BALTO

Cleveland Museum of Natural History

LEONARD SEPPALA, FRITZ & TOGO ABOARD STEAMSHIP, SEATTLE 1926

Museum of History and Industry; Post Intelligencer Collection

town, and moved into their special quarters at the Brookside Zoo (now known as the Cleveland Metroparks Zoo). Over 15,000 people came the first day to see the dogs in their new enclosure. Balto enjoyed his years there and died March 14, 1933. He was preserved at the Cleveland Museum of Natural History where he can be seen on display today.

Seppala, even though he had raised Balto, always felt disappointed that the heroics of his beloved Togo were not sufficiently recognized. He believed that Balto had erroneously been proclaimed a hero by overzealous reporters. After all, Togo had led his team through the longest and most difficult leg of the journey. He had kept his team on the trail during gale force winds and near whiteout conditions. He had given his all, worn himself out and his best sledding days were over. The team had traveled 170 miles in just three days to pick up the serum, then turned around and raced another 91 miles back toward Nome. It was an incredible achievement.

Another unsung hero was Togo's half-brother, Fritz. He was a light cream-colored dog who ran alongside Togo during the serum run. He had beautiful gray and brown markings and Seppala always referred to him as "a great dog."

In the fall of 1926, Seppala took Togo, Fritz and 41 other dogs south on his own tour of the United States. They made hundreds of appearances, the highlight being a 10-day exhibition at New York's Madison Square Garden. The famous Antarctic and Arctic explorer Roald Amundsen delivered a speech in Togo's honor. Then, to the delight of the crowd of over 20,000 people, Seppala's fellow Norwegian also awarded Togo with a gold medal. Togo had finally been given the recognition he deserved.

Togo and his fellow dogs finally found a new home in Maine where they demonstrated the breed's strengths and abilities and helped procreate new generations of quality dogs.

In 1930, partly as a result of the newfound popularity after the serum run, and Seppala's influence, the American Kennel Club officially recognized the Siberian Husky breed. Unlike Balto who had been "neutered" as a pup, Togo and Fritz went on to sire many pups. It is said that most of the Siberian Huskies today can be traced back to the rugged intelligent dogs who took part in the great serum run of 1925.

Togo who had been born in October, 1913, passed on December 5, 1929, in Maine. He was preserved and returned to Alaska where he can be seen at the Iditarod Trail Sled Race Museum in Wasilla, Alaska. Fritz was also mounted and eventually made it back to Nome, where he is displayed at the Carrie McLain museum.

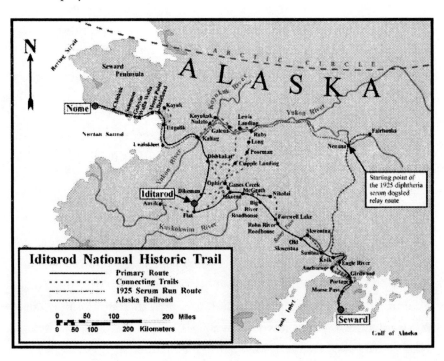

The annual Iditarod Trail Sled Dog Race is held every March to commemorate the historic "Great Race of Mercy," to honor the memory of the heroes, and to remind people today of the value of inoculations against horrible diseases. One of the world's most grueling sporting events, it stretches from Anchorage to Nome and covers over 1,200 miles, testing athletes and dogs from all over the world.

SEPPALA POSES WITH THREE SIBERIAN HUSKIES

Harry T. Becker Photograph Collection; Harry T. Becker Photographer
Alaska State Library Historical Collections

Thousands of years ago when man came across the land bridge that connected Asia with North America he brought his companions, his dogs. For thousands of years the native cultures had a mutually dependent partnership of survival. They struggled together and depended on each other for life itself in a harsh brutal world.

When you visit Central Park and look at the statue of Balto, you'll see a great dog that performed heroically under the worst conditions. You should also think about all the men and other dogs that gave their best to help a small town in peril. But the statue represents even more than that. It was one of the last times that we relied on our friend the dog under those conditions.

The sled and dog team have now been replaced by airplanes and snowmobiles. When you see that monument you'll also be reminded of an ancient relationship and a bygone era, not very long ago that we have traded in for something seemingly better. We now mostly rely on our new technologies. Maybe in the name of progress we have traded in the best friend we ever had.

BALTO'S MONUMENT

OWNEY

The dog that went Postal

Some dogs become famous for different reasons; an amazing feat, saving lives, a display of extraordinary intelligence, or perhaps for taking part in an historical event. Our next story is about an ordinary small mongrel dog that was adopted by United States postal workers and came to be their beloved partner. During his career he was known as Owney, the "Railway Postal Clerk's Mascot." Mail carriers, who travel around in a uniform carrying a bag into strange neighborhoods have historically been the arch enemy of protective dogs everywhere. This is the story of one dog who loved the mailman.

Owney became a regular at the Albany, New York Post Office sometime in 1888. He was a half-starved, scruffy little terrier mix with one bad eye, hoping to get out of the cold. One night he wandered into the local Post Office and found a place to sleep on the pile of mailbags. Because the postal workers there were kind to him, fed him, and gave him shelter, he soon became attached to the sight and smell of postal bags, mail and postal employees. At some

OWNEY AND CLERK

Smithsonian National Postal Museum

Owney

point the adventurous little Owney started riding the mail wagon down to the main train station. He soon had the nerve to board the train with the mail and then one fateful day he was invited along for a trip.

In 1888 the Railway Mail Service was the main method of transporting and delivering mail across the nation. For over 100 years, from the Civil War until the last run in 1977, mail traveled on trains. Specially built railroad cars allowed the mail to be sorted onboard as it crisscrossed the country. Teams of clerks would cancel, sort and load the mail into each town's bags, while they were moving toward their destination. These men were the elite of the postal system and it was an exciting yet dangerous job.

The system provided prompt delivery and pickup service for large cities and small towns alike. Even in places where the train did not stop the mail went through. A unique system was designed where they would hang the mailbag near the train tracks and it could be grabbed or dropped off by a hook as the train went speeding by.

The Railroad Post Office handled the majority of U.S. Mail for decades. This was a time before telephones, airplanes and electricity. Railroad was the fastest and most efficient method of transportation. The rail network extended to the far reaches of North America, and the men took pride in delivering the mail quickly under the most adverse circumstances. Today we enjoy a world of cell phones, computers, satellites and instant electronic access to people worldwide. Sometimes we forget how important communication by letter was. Processing mail and mail service was so vital, and of such national importance, that mail clerks were exempt from the draft during times of war.

It was very dangerous work delivering mail by train. The old wooden railroad cars that followed behind steam powered locomotives were firetraps. Bad weather, fire, train wrecks and even robberies were a very real danger. For example between 1890 and 1905, 143 postal clerks lost their lives in incidents on the trains.

OWNEY POSES WITH HIS FRIENDS

Smithsonian National Postal Museum

Owney's attachment to mail soon had him riding aboard the mail trains and becoming their mascot. A mascot is a person, animal or an object that is adopted by a group as a symbol of good luck. Amazingly no train Owney rode in was ever involved in a wreck. Owney was their good luck charm.

If Owney was in a traveling mood when the mail was sent down to the station he would jump on the wagon and hitch a ride. He would wait until the last bag was thrown aboard, and when he made his decision, he would jump aboard, bark a good-bye and take off with the train. From there Owney was the guest of the postal clerks, who always looked after him. He would travel back and forth, and his trips got longer and longer, but he would always return to his friends and home in Albany. When someone asked the postmaster how the clerks knew when Owney was traveling, the answer was "When the cat comes in the office we know that Owney is away."

Eventually Owney traveled farther and farther on his train trips. The workers in Albany gave him a special collar with his name on it for identification and if necessary to help him get him sent back home. The collar was inscribed '**Owney, Albany Post Office, New York.**' He also traveled with a log book to help keep track of his travels. The lovable little dog was often given mail bag tokens and other items to hang on his new collar by employees of nearly every place he visited. Soon Owney had too many souvenirs and mementos of his travels to carry around on his collar. When he would return to Albany they would gather and save his mementos. Owney was becoming famous along the mail routes. The Railway Post Office workers were his family.

As a result of his many trips, Owney became well known among the Postal employees along the line. The Postmaster General John Wanamaker eventually took notice of, appreciated and admired the little dog. He presented Owney with a special harness to help hold his medals. He carried so many that he would jingle when he walked. Occasionally there was need to lighten his load and the

POSTAL CLERKS AT WORK ON TRAIN

Smithsonian National Postal Museum

WRECKED MAIL TRAIN

Smithsonian National Postal Museum

Posing with His Medals

Smithsonian National Postal Museum

extra medals would be sent back to Albany or Washington, DC for safekeeping.

To earn his keep Owney helped out at Post Office events. In October 1892, he was 'on daily exhibition' at the Post Office Employees fair at Madison Square Garden. While there he greeted his fans and helped raise money to start a pension fund for New York Postal employees.

In 1894 Owney traveled once again to New Orleans, where he enjoyed the hospitality for which the town is famous. He was escorted through town and attended the World's Fair during his stay. Owney had traveled to every large city in the United States. If the train went there Owney did too. Some places he visited included Dallas, Seattle, Louisville, Nashville, Pontiac, Cloverdale, Houston, Kansas city, Memphis, and Fort Worth, just to name a few.

In 1895 the Postmaster of Tacoma, Washington sent him as a "registered dog package," on a very long and special trip. He traveled around the world as an ambassador of the U.S. Postal Service. He started his overseas adventure by being tagged and shipped out on the steamship Victoria. He left from Tacoma, on August 19, 1895. He was so special that he had his own personal assistant to look out for him. Before he left, the Postmaster A.C. Case attached a note to his collar which read as follows:

> *To all who may meet this dog: Owney is his name. He is the pet of 100,000 Postal employees of the United States of America. He started to-day August 19, 1895, for a trip around the world. Treat him kindly and speed him on his journey across ocean and land to Yokohama, Hong Kong and New York. From New York send him overland to Tacoma, and who knows he may compass the globe and beat the record of Nellie Bly and George Francis Train and be known as a celebrated globetrotter?*

In October 1895 the New York Times interviewed the purser

who looked after Owney on the Victoria, Mr. Wood. It was learned that Owney had been left in Kobe, Japan after he had enjoyed a very warm reception. It had been decided not to leave him in China as was originally planned. While in Hong Kong, the captain of the ship had presented him with a nice silver medal, for his growing collection, inscribed with names of the officers of the ship. When off the ship, Owney enjoyed running around behind the rickshaws but the locals there really did not take a shine to him. Since dogs are eaten in many Asian countries it was probably wise to leave him in Japan instead. The Japanese love their dogs. The Mikado of Japan presented him with a special silver medal emblazoned with the Japanese Coat of Arms.

From Japan, Owney continued on his long journey. He passed through the Indian Ocean, the Suez Canal, the Mediterranean and stopped and visited many ports and exotic destinations along the way including Algiers and the Azores. He then crossed the Atlantic and returned to New York City aboard the steamer Port Phillip. There was quite a reception upon his arrival back in New York. People had been following the furry adventurer and his journey in the newspapers. The Captain hated to part with lovable Owney. He had made new friends aboard the ship and it is said that he single handedly rid the vessel of every rat onboard. He was delivered as addressed to the New York Post Office by the Captain himself. Owney was covered in newly acquired medals and tags. From there he was once again 'mailed' and put aboard a train west.

His circumnavigation of the globe was complete when he returned to Tacoma by train December 29, 1895, 132 days after he had departed. He was met at the station by his old friend Mr. Wood of the Victoria. He had not set a world record but it was still quite an accomplishment for a dog. During his traveling years he crisscrossed the United States many times and also traveled north to Canada and Alaska and possibly all the way south to Mexico City. It is said that in his lifetime he traveled over 140,000 miles with the mail on his many journeys.

Owney was famous and was welcome almost everywhere he went. But not everyone appreciated the apparently scroungy little traveler. In April of 1897 he had a bad experience in Chicago. Despite our pups' travels, fame and achievements, when the Superintendent there heard of Owney's arrival he issued an edict that the little dog was not to receive transport in his district. In banning what he considered to be a free loading mutt he was quoted in the paper as follows:

If the dog were in any ways remarkable for his intelligence there might be some reason for paying attention to him. He is only a mongrel cur, which has been petted until the thing has become disgusting. His riding around on the postal cars distracts the attention of the clerks, takes up the time of the employees at stations in showing him around, and it is about time he is kicked out.

Ouch! Fortunately for Owney most people did not feel this way. When referred to as an unwanted package or when he was ignored he took it in stride and tried to make friends where he was welcome.

Living nearby in Albany was a canine contemporary of Owney. He was large grey Scottish Terrier by the name of Railroad Jack. His story is very similar and he and Owney knew each other and were friends. Like Owney he was a traveling dog. He also went by train around the United States, to Mexico and even Canada. Apparently people in Albany loved to launch their mascots out into the world and delighted in the interesting souvenirs they would return with. Along his thousands of miles of travels he collected metal tags, medals and even a tomahawk and souvenir knives. He wore a collar to tell where he came from and would always be returned back to his home at Union Depot in Albany where his friends were waiting for him.

Railroad Jack also had an interesting and fitting name for a dog that made a career around trains. A railroad jack is a tool used to lift up railroad cars to work on them. Owney and Jack had their differences.

OWNEY ON EXHIBIT

Owney lived at the Post Office, was loyal to postal employees and only traveled in mail cars. Jack lived in the Albany baggage room of the Wells Fargo Express Company; he traveled in the baggage car of the train and found his friends in the express messengers who he followed and obeyed. Like many of us, Jack had gradually grown a little stout over the years. On returning from one of his trips there was this message attached to his collar:

Since Jack started out on his trip with the boys he hasn't lost much of avoirdupois, though burdened with twenty-odd pounds of fat, just notice his movements when you call 'a rat.'

Jack's rat catching and traveling days came to a quiet end in June, 1893. He had just eaten his dinner when he returned to his room and laid down and died. He received a nice article in the New York Times announcing his passing. Plans were made to preserve his body but I am not sure if that ever happened and if it did where it would be now. Fame is fickle and while few have ever heard of Jack, his friend Owney is a different story.

Owney died under somewhat clouded circumstances June 11, 1897. He had traveled to Toledo, Ohio and had been tied up in the basement awaiting a local news photographer. Owney did not like the predicament, fought his chain, and became very upset. Efforts to calm him down resulted in him biting a postal worker. During that era, fear of hydrophobia in dogs was a very serious concern. That fear resulted in Owney being "put to sleep" or shot.

When word reached his friends in Albany they were understandably upset. Postal employees raised money to have him preserved and after many years on display at the Post Office in Washington, DC he was transferred to the Smithsonian in 1911. Owney had collected 1,017 tags in his career, traveled thousands of miles and brought happiness to many hard working men who enjoyed having a little dog to travel with. While not a handsome dog, he was kind and intelligent. He was

Smithsonian National Postal Museum

devotedly attached to his friends. It was not rabies or a gunshot that took his life, it was human ignorance.

A forever stamp was issued in his memory on July 27, 2011, leading to renewed awareness of this lovable mutt. Several books have been written about Owney and his adventures, mostly for children who love to hear his story. He is now on display at the National Postal Museum, in the atrium, still proudly wearing his collar and harness with many of his souvenir medals and tags attached. If they ever decide to move him I hope he goes by train.

OWNEY THE POSTAL DOG ©2011

CHAPTER 11

SWANSEA JACK

Ne'er had mankind more faithful friend...

ales is a small coastal country on the Atlantic Ocean and the Irish Sea. It is located on the southwest side of the island of Great Britain and is a member of the United Kingdom. The hero of our next story is a handsome large black retriever with a wavy fur coat and long bushy tail. The retriever breeds of dog love to chase and bring back objects, especially in the water. These attributes all combined to make our hero a very special famous dog that will be remembered for years to come.

Our story begins along the waterfront docks of the Welsh town of Swansea. The people here found their identity in the seafront, the river and the docks. One of the most well-known sons of Swansea is the writer Dylan Thomas. A hard working town, it had the location, facilities and manpower to export the raw materials that had been the fuel of the Industrial Revolution. Some of the main exports were wine, hides, wool, cloth, coal and especially copper. In fact, so much copper was processed in the 18th and 19th centuries that the area

JACK SWIMMING AT THE DOCK

Treboeth History Society

became known as "Copperopolis." The great depression of the early 20th century hit this area hard and marked the end of an era for this once thriving port. Amidst the high unemployment, poverty and steady decline there was a bright spot. A furry hero emerged who help keep the people's spirits aloft.

Born sometime in 1930, the dog, Jack, was owned by a gentleman named William Thomas, a Swansea native. Mariners from this port town had a good reputation and were well respected. As a reflection of their seafaring heritage the people of Swansea were given the nickname of 'Jack.' Most likely given because of the jack-tarred apparel mariners wore as protection from extreme conditions at sea. It turned out to be the perfect name for this dog that would someday make the town proud.

Jack and William lived in the heart of the docklands in the North Dock/River Tawe area a few feet from the waterfront. The local children would frequently gather along the docks and have fun playing and swimming. The fun just gets better when a local happy dog joins in and you can all play together. But while Jack loved to play with the kids he was afraid of the water. One day William and the kids pushed him in. Jack quickly overcame his fear and happily discovered his breed's purpose in life. His newfound love of swimming and the water would change many lives.

One day in June 1931, while swimming near the docks, Jack grabbed a young 12 year old boy who was in danger of drowning and pulled him to shore. No one really took much notice at the time, but a few weeks later our heroic dog rescued another swimmer who was suffering from a cramp. This time a crowd was there to witness the event. The story quickly spread and the local paper reported the deed. On July 7th, 1931 the South Wales Daily Post ran the story as a front page headline. In appreciation, Swansea Town awarded the now well-known dog a leather and silver collar to honor his rescues. Jack had quickly become a local celebrity. He displayed all those attributes we love in our pets, courage and loyalty combined with a friendly playful nature.

But our pup was just getting started in his life saving career. Within a few months he saved a man from Liverpool who had fallen from the docks. Apparently he would respond to cries for help by diving in and pulling the victim back to the dock or riverbank. Jack turned his breed's instinct to retrieve into an obsession for pulling troubled swimmers from the water. He kept so busy and was so vigilant that by August of 1934 he was credited by his owner with 14 rescues.

Jack was duly honored with a lifetime membership in the amusingly named 'Tail Waggers Club' whose motto was "I Help My Pals." The club had been formed to promote canine welfare. They also presented him with a special medallion to wear on his collar. The silver medal featured the club's whimsical emblem; two crossed tails on one side with the motto and the name and address of Jack's owner on the other. This organization existed to promote the general welfare of dogs and provided education and assistance to dog owners. They also helped raise money to help train guide dogs for the blind and helped support the Glasgow Veterinary Training College.

When he wasn't busy saving people, Jack was taken about to help raise money for local charities. He soon became a fixture at parades, carnivals, sporting events and other civic gatherings. He was outfitted with a specially made harness that carried two collection boxes, one on each side. Escorted by his owner or his friends (the local children), he would wander about these events and collect the money. His fame and popularity helped him to collect much needed funds for the Tail Waggers, the blind, local hospitals, the YMCA, Poppies for British Legion, Adult Deaf, the Peoples Dispensary for Sick Animals, and many other appreciative worthy organizations.

Jack and his owner enjoyed their newfound popularity around town. Their cold damp dwelling at the docks was soon replaced by a permanent residence at the nice warm Victoria Hotel. Jack thrived on the attention of his new friends and enjoyed the camaraderie of the other guests and pleasant evening gatherings at the hotel bar. One special lifetime buddy was Jack Gordon whose parents ran the hotel.

SOLICITING FOR CHARITY

Treboeth History Society

He was a young boy and he and Jack spent many happy days together. Old photos of the dog show him and Jack playing and fundraising together. Years later Jack would tell the stories about his famous friend. The people of town were quite fond of their local celebrity dog and he was now proudly referred to as Swansea Jack.

In his spare time Jack would wander around and patrol the docks and area beaches acting as self-appointed lifeguard looking for trouble. Most of the people that he rescued were children or seamen; children who could not yet swim well and sailors who got into trouble returning from the local taverns. On July 8, 1935, the evening paper announced that Jack had made his twentieth save. A man washing his hands had slipped into the water, and not being able to swim, quickly found himself in serious trouble. Jack plunged in and pulled him safely to shore while a large crowd watched. Jack's story was spreading and he was becoming a nationally known celebrity.

In September of 1935, Jack was publically honored by the Mayor of Swansea. The Peoples Dispensary for Sick Animals presented Jack with an inscribed Silver Shield. It commemorated his recent 21st save, a young child. Another highlight of the event was when the National Canine Defense League gave our hero their highest award, a bronze medal, regarded as the Canine V.C. He would receive this special medal two separate times. No other dog had ever had that honor. The South Wales Evening Post carried the story, including a photograph of the gathered dignitaries in front of the Guildhall steps. The headlines in the paper announced:

Mayor Decorates Hero at the Guildhall
Canine V.C. for Swansea Jack
Dog That Has Saved 21 Lives

People would gather down at the docks to catch a glimpse of and photograph Jack. The happy story had spread across the nation. He

Treboeth History Society

was loved by everyone. He continued to receive many more trophies, medals and citations from various groups. In 1936 he was named "Bravest Dog of the Year" by the local Star newspaper. The shield and the other medallions he received found a place in a new specially made harness. Worn on his back, it allowed him to display his many awards when he attended special events.

By popular demand, Swansea Jack and his owner started traveling by train to some of the largest and well known dog shows across the country. In fact much of their time was now devoted to public appearances; the people of Great Britain love their dogs. They soon became well known seasoned travelers. On one of their excursions he was awarded and presented a Silver Cup by the Lord Mayor of London. One of the biggest and most exclusive events they visited was the prestigious Crufts Show, regularly attended by "top dogs" and dignitaries including the British Royal Family.

When not traveling, Jack would resume his happy routine at home. The local and national newspapers would regularly run articles detailing the latest rescue and kept a running count of how many lives he had saved.

At some point William and Jack moved to Roger Street in neighboring Treboeth and lived with William's family. They were now living a few miles away from the waterfront but Jack still managed to find his way down to the docks and beach to visit and look around. Jack also found time to sire a few litters of pups. People were hopeful that another hero would emerge from his progeny but despite efforts to train them for water rescue, not one ever showed Jack's aptitude for life saving.

On September 3rd, 1936 Swansea Jack made his last recorded rescue. Hearing cries of distress from the beach, Jack bounded over the dunes and headed to the water. He swam out and found the swimmer who was calling for help. Witnessed by a large crowd he had saved his 27th life. The national daily paper featured the following headline:

SWANSEA JACK AND WILLIAM THOMAS

TAILWAGGERS CLUB TRUST

The Daily Mirror
League of Kindness to Animals.
(Brave Dogs' Roll of Honour.)

This is to Certify that *Swansea Jack*
owned by *Mrs W Thomas*
of *Victoria Hotel, College Street, Swansea*
has been placed on the **Roll of Honour** for **Conspicuous Bravery**
and **Faithful Service.**

*Swansea Jack has been responsible for the saving
of twenty one persons from drowning, as in so far
hath spared.*

Swansea's Wonder Dog Makes 27th Rescue

Jack's idyllic life was full of adventure and a lot of fun, but all good things must come to an end. Jack passed away on October 2, 1937; sadly he had accidentally ingested some type of rat poison and died at only 7 years old. Bill Thomas had lost his best friend. The news of Jack's death appeared in newspapers across the country. People were sad but also upset. It was illegal and irresponsible to place poison where it might be accessed by domestic animals. The National Canine Defence League printed and put up posters offering a reward to try and find the person or persons who were carelessly using poison to kill vermin. The culprit was never found.

Jack had enjoyed a good life with plenty of affection and was loved by his owner and many friends. They all missed him and there was an outpouring of grief and also anger for the way he died. It was so sad that such a special nice dog in his prime had been taken prematurely from them. Letters poured in and were published in the newspapers remembering the brave dog, telling their 'Jack' stories and sharing their affection for the heroic lovable dog. One especially eloquent and interesting letter printed in the paper was the following poem;

I 'aint any sort of a writer,
For writin' I 'aint got the knack:
I'm just a poor ignorant blighter,
Wot's grateful to old Swansea Jack.
One bleak chilly day in November,
To my ship I was on my way back;
'Tis a day I shall always remember,
And the debt I owe brave Swansea Jack.
My mind was bemused I suppose, sir
All night I'd been spending my cash,

£25 REWARD

DOG POISONING

The above reward will be paid for information leading to the conviction of the person or persons who have illegally laid down poison without preventing access thereto by dogs and other domestic animals, as required by the law.

THE REWARD WILL BE PAID BY

THE NATIONAL CANINE DEFENCE LEAGUE,
VICTORIA STATION HOUSE, LONDON, S.W.1.

Treboeth History Society

I stumbled, and right in I goes, sir,
And no one I thought 'eard the splash,
I yelled as I came up for breath, sir,
There wasn't a soul on the quay;
If drownin's a nice easy death, sir,
It 'aint wot it's cracked up to be!
I 'ardly know much of the rest, sir,
My mind was a sort of a fog;
I felt somethin' pawing' my chest, sir,
Then felt myself seized by a dog.
If in 'Eaven a place can't be found, sir,
For creatures so noble an' fine;
I'd willingly rot in the ground, sir,
If I knew Swansea Jack could have mine!
　　　　　　—Huan Mee

The writer was not alone with his feelings. Many people owed their lives to this beautiful black 'wonder dog.' A deluge of suggestions poured in about the best way to honor the fallen hero. Of course people wanted to erect a permanent memorial to their special dog. Meetings and discussions were held. It was decided to bury the dog and build a monument in a place of honor on the Swansea Promenade where it would be very visible to the public. Donations came in locally and from as far away as Canada, New Zealand and South Africa. They collected more than enough money and commissioned a beautiful grey Penzance granite memorial. It features a large bas relief of Jack's head and one of his medals. The monument was unveiled one year after his death. Local dignitaries, family and many friends attended the ceremony. The statue is there today. It is inscribed as follows:

Erected to the Memory of
Swansea Jack
The Brave Retreiver Who Saved 27 Human
and Two Canine Lives From Drowning
Loved and Mourned by All Dog Lovers
Died October 2nd 1937 at the Age of Seven Years

Ne'er Had Mankind More Faithful Friend
Than Thou
Who Oft Thy Life Did'st Lend
To Save Some Human Soul From Death

Years later some people cast doubt on Jack's exploits. In response more testimonials were gathered. Including the following letter published in the Daily Mirror, November 1966;

I am one of the people Swansea Jack pulled out of the docks. When
I was cycling to work along the dock on December 23rd 1936,
something caught my front wheel. In I went bike and all. I could
not swim nor could I get out of the dock. Along came Jack and
pulled me to the steps, where his owner dragged me out. To this
day when I go to Swansea I always go to Jack's memorial stone
to thank him. The bike belonged to my sister and thanks to the
Swansea docks police, the bike was retrieved to me. You could also
see Jack collecting for charity with a box on his back. I'm sure he
used to collect more than anyone.
John. F. Griffiths,-Cwmbran Monmouthshire

Since his death there have been news articles, a few books and in 1979 there was even a song written about the life and adventures of Swansea Jack. In 2000 the New Found Friends of Bristol, a group

SOME OF JACK'S MANY AWARDS

Treboeth History Society

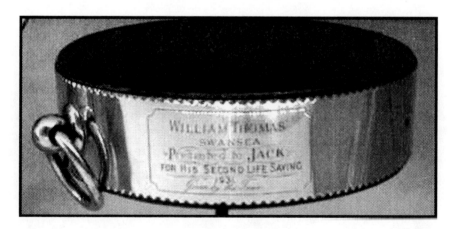

Jack's **COLLAR**

Treboeth History Society

that trains dogs for aquatic rescue, named Jack 'Dog of the Century'. Jack's monument is still standing today on the Promenade near St. Helen's Rugby Ground. It has been over 75 years since he lived and now a new generation passes by his monument and wonders who he was. It has been many years but when they hear the story, the legend of Swansea Jack, a 'monumental dog' lives on.

SWANSEA JACK MONUMENT

CHAPTER 12

SEA DOG BAMSE

...to remember the loyalty and friendship...

—Prince Andrew

Norway lies along the sea in the western part of Scandinavia in Northern Europe. It is bordered by Sweden, Denmark and Russia to the east and the sea on the south, west and north. The thousands of islands, deep fjords, glaciers, mountains and lakes all combine to make up what is arguably some of the most visually impressive scenery in the world. National Geographic has listed the Norwegian fjords as the world's top tourist attraction. The wide variety of topography and climate make it one of the planet's most biodiverse locations. Norway's high latitude and location on the Arctic Circle have also earned it the nickname 'Land of the Midnight Sun.' This economically stable and resource rich country was rocked by the events of the Second World War. Despite the desire to stay neutral the country was forced to fight for survival. A large lovable

SHIP'S DOG BAMSE

Courtesy: Montrose Heritage Trust

dog is gratefully remembered for his role in keeping the Norwegian spirits aloft through the conflict.

Erling Hafto was the harbor-master of Honningsvåg, located on the North Cape island of Magerøya at the far northern tip of Norway, a remote town 1600 kilometers north of Oslo. He had everything a man could ask for, his wife Halldis, a nice home, a good job and a growing family. His job required him to occasionally leave the family for a few weeks and travel back to Oslo, where he had been born, to file reports to the government. On one such trip in 1937 he returned from the long trip with a special gift for the family, a puppy. Their four children, ages nine to one were the girls Kjersti, Torbjør, Vigdis and the son Gunnar-Hedge. There are few better fun combinations than children and a puppy, and this was an especially beautiful furry little dog. He was a Saint Bernard, a rarity in this country but well suited for the northern climate and cuddling with children.

The family soon decided to name him Bamse (pronounced 'Bump-sa') meaning bear or teddy bear. Bamse grew to be a kind and gentle dog. He would play with and look after the children. On one scary occasion when two year old Vigdis was deathly ill, Bamse protectively stayed by her side for twelve days and nights. He seemed to sense the seriousness of the situation and kept everyone away except her mother and the doctor. She seemed doomed but recovered and the family always gave the dog some of the credit. The children later recollected how he protectively acted as a nanny and while at play he was always gentle and would allow the children to climb on him for a ride.

Their idyllic life took an unexpected turn when the Germans began to threaten the freedom they enjoyed. Erling Hafto was recruited to come back into the Royal Norwegian Navy as Captain of the Thorodd. The Thorodd (whale catcher) was an aging whaling ship that had been converted and drafted into service as a coastal patrol boat to help with the escalating hostilities. With the Captain came his dog, Bamse. Leaving Halldis at home alone to take care of

4 children was bad enough without leaving her with a giant dog to take care of also. In February 1940, the full grown 100 kilo dog was brought on board as a registered crewmember, and became perhaps the largest dog who ever served as a ship's mascot.

The Nazis invaded Norway in April of 1940 and by June had taken over the country. Fortunately, King Haakon and members of the Norwegian government were able to escape by boat to London. The Thorodd was one of only 13 navy vessels to help and also escape to the U.K. For the duration of the war the King was able to broadcast inspirational messages to his countrymen. This helped inspire the Norwegian resistance movement to their civil disobedience and resistance to the German occupiers. Some Norwegians fought as part of the Free Norwegian Forces and many joined the Allied Forces. The country's large merchant marine fleet was very important to the Allied war effort and helped at every sea operation from Dunkirk to Normandy.

The Thorodd was then converted to a minesweeper and was stationed in Montrose and Dundee, Scotland for the duration of the war. Bamse became a special shipmate for the crew. Minesweeping is nerve wracking hazardous work. Bamse would stand at the foremost gun tower and showed courage while the ship was underway. The crew even fashioned him a special helmet to wear. He quickly became essential to the ships morale. In September 1940 the Captain was reassigned to a new ship, and intended to take his dog with him. The crew confronted him and said he could not take "their" dog with him. They threatened that they would not return to sea without him. The captain decided to loan the dog to the ship until the war was over.

The Thorodd was often in port for a week or two. Bamse enjoyed traveling into town with or without his shipmates. The men made him his own navy hat to wear which certainly gave him a lovable yet official look. With dignity he would visit the pubs, shops and local bakeries in hopes of a friendly handout. He would usually wait

BAMSE AND CAPTAIN OSCAR

Courtesy: Montrose Heritage Trust

READY FOR BATTLE!

Courtesy: Montrose Heritage Trust

outside the bars while the crew would go inside for a drink. His nanny instinct would have him round up and nudge them back to the ship before curfew. He was also known to act as sentry on the ship and would not allow anyone unknown to come aboard.

One tale that added to his legend was the night he may have saved a crew member's life. While out on a walk, one of the ship's officers was confronted by a man with a knife who intended to rob hm. From a distance Bamse saw what was happening and ran up to the attacker and pushed him away from the officer. During the course of the scuffle Bamse eventually pushed the man into the water and the danger was over. On another occasion some crewmembers were talking and suddenly heard a splash followed by loud incessant dog barking. A member of the crew had fallen overboard and Bamse had jumped in after him. The dog was able to keep him afloat until the other crewmembers came and helped them both back into the ship.

One time he joined the men inside a pub. Ignoring the house cat lounging on the bar, he jumped up on his hind legs, rested his large paws on the bar, pushed the cat aside and waited while the bartender filled him a bowl of beer to enjoy with his mates.

Sometimes he would use his size to break up fights amongst his shipmates by rearing up on his hind legs and placing his paws and weight on the offender's shoulders. Bamse learned to ride the bus around town with his shipmates. He finally learned where to stand and wait for the bus all by himself. The bus driver would open the door and the big dog would climb aboard and knew enough to head upstairs for his ride because dogs were not allowed on the lower level. That was fine but his fare became an issue. The crew purchased him a pass which he wore around his neck. The bus drivers would pick him up and let him off while he made his rounds around town looking for food and his shipmates. He was always sure to get them back to the ship on time. He became well known in town and loved to attend football games and play with the local children.

He started as mascot for the KNM Thorodd, became the mascot

for the Norwegian Navy and in 1944 was designated an official Allied Forces Mascot by the People's Dispensary for Sick Animals (PDSA) and named, "The Largest Dog in the Allied Forces." His face wearing his sailor's hat was sent out as Christmas cards to the Norwegian forces around the world.

Bamse died peacefully along the Montrose waterfront near the ship in July 1944. His big heart gave out; he was only 7 years old. He had become a symbol of freedom for his country, and had made many friends. When the day arrived, all Montrose came to a halt for the funeral. He was buried with full military honors by the sea and facing Norway in the sand dunes near the South Esk River. Businesses closed and several hundred people, including schoolchildren, Norwegian sailors, Allied servicemen, shopkeepers and others from town who loved the special dog lined the way and joined in the funeral procession.

Their common war interactions and feeling for this dog helped cement an enduring special relationship and appreciation between the people of Norway and the Scots. The Norwegians also appreciated the British assistance during the dark war years. In remembrance they give a gift of a Christmas tree every year that is erected in London's Trafalgar Square. To their friends the Scots, they give a tree that is displayed in the City of Edinburgh.

Bamse was awarded the Norges Hundeorden in 1984 by the Norwegian Animal Protection Association, Dyrebeskyttelsen, for his inspirational service. After carefully gathering all the evidence he was also the recipient of the Peoples Dispensary for Sick Animals (PDSA) Gold Medal for Gallantry (2006), Britain's highest award for animal heroism.

On October 17, 2006 the Duke of York, His Royal Highness Prince Andrew, unveiled a larger than life bronze statue of Bamse on Wharf Street in Montrose. Representatives of the Royal Norwegian Navy and the British Navy attended the ceremony. Some of Prince Andrew's remarks included the following; "...the people of the

SHIPMATES AT FUNERAL

Courtesy: Montrose Heritage Trust

Courtesy: Montrose Heritage Trust

MONUMENT DEDICATION WITH PRINCE ANDREW

Courtesy: Montrose Heritage Trust

Norwegian Navy, the people of the Royal Navy and the people of Montrose hold this dog in the highest esteem." It was special day and among the special guests at the unveiling was Vigdis Hafto, one of the children who had been given the little puppy almost 70 years before.

In June, 2009, one more identical statue was unveiled in Honningsvåg, Norway, Bamse's hometown. The local schoolchildren were joined by children from Scotland for the well-attended ceremony. To make the celebration even more special the visitors were even accompanied by a pipe band! Symbolically the statue in Honningsvåg faces southwest toward Montrose while the statue in Montrose faces northeast to Honningsvåg. Another smaller version of the statue was displayed at the Imperial War Museum in London before being sent to the Maritime Museum in Horten, Norway in 2007.

A nice book "Sea Dog Bamse, World War II Canine Hero" written by Andrew Orr and Angus Whitson has become a very popular best seller and tells the story of Bamse in detail. The Montrose Heritage Trust has been instrumental in keeping the memory of the dog alive. Bamse reflected the psyche of the Norwegian people perfectly. As the heroic mascot of the Free Norwegian Forces he became the country's national hero and symbol of freedom during the war. They both desired to live gently and in peace but when cornered and forced into a fight they responded, and their Viking spirit was unleashed until the job was done.

IN SCOTLAND LOOKING TOWARD NORWAY

Courtesy: Montrose Heritage Trust

BAMSE AND ADMIRER

Courtesy: Montrose Heritage Trust

BAMSE PROJECT LOGO

Courtesy: Montrose Heritage Trust

CHAPTER 13

PATSY ANN

Sittin' in the morning sun
I'll be sittin' when the evening comes
Watching the ships roll in
Then I watch them roll away again, yeah...

—Otis Redding

If you ever take a cruise to Alaska you are very likely to run into our next monumental dog, Patsy Ann. She'll be sitting quietly on the dock facing the sea and waiting for your arrival. This homely little Bull Terrier won't bark or beg for scraps anymore, since she is now a beautiful bronze statue.

Juneau, the capital of Alaska is only accessible by air or sea. It has become a very popular cruise ship destination visited by over a million passengers every year. People enjoy the history, the Native American culture, and the beautiful scenery such as the nearby Mendenhall Glacier.

The native Tlingit Indians inhabited the area for thousands of

PATSY ANN

Butler/Dale Photographic Collection, Evelyn I. Butler Photographer

The official greeter at Juneau

Mary Nan Gamble Photograph collection
Willis T. Gasman Photographer–Alaska State Library historical Collection

years and the waterfront around Juneau was one of their favorite fishing grounds. The nearly 600,000 square miles of Alaskan territory was acquired by the United States from Russia in 1868 for the price of $7,200,000. In 1880 Tlingit Chief Kowee directed Joe Juneau and Richard Harris to the head of Gold Creek where they found gold nuggets "as large as peas and beans." They marked off 160 acres and a mining camp soon appeared. Within a year a small town had formed. The town prospered, the population grew and in 1906 Juneau was named the territorial capital. The new state of Alaska was admitted to the Union as the 49th state in 1959.

Patsy Ann was born October 12, 1929, in Portland, Oregon. Probably stone-deaf since birth, this purebred white English Bull Terrier was shipped north to Alaska destined to be a family pet for a Juneau dentist, Dr. Keyser. She later went to live with another family but over the years she became owned by no one and everyone, an independent wandering citizen of the town. Her shelter of choice was the local longshoreman's hall.

Patsy Ann was known to scurry down to the dock and meet every ship that arrived. Although deaf she somehow not only knew when the ship was coming but also at which dock. People would see her making her move and follow her knowing the ship was getting close. Once the ship arrived she would greet the passengers as they came down the gangplank. Patsy Ann lapped up the petting, attention and treats she would receive with the confident attitude that she deserved every bit of it. She would also wander along the dock sniffing for the galley porthole knowing a few more tidbits might be handed out. On occasion she was seen swimming out to boats anchored in the harbor just to make sure all arrivals received their greeting.

In 1934 the Mayor proclaimed Patsy Ann the 'Official Greeter of Juneau, Alaska'. She was thereafter exempted from the licensing law and allowed to roam the town at will. The local stevedores commissioned and paid for an artist to make her a special leather collar to wear. Patsy Ann would wander freely around town visiting and making friends at hotels, bars. She even paraded up and down the aisles at the local movie theater, probably looking for a snack. At some point she left her paw prints for posterity in a newly poured sidewalk on South Seward Street.

It remains a mystery as to exactly how a deaf dog could correctly anticipate arriving vessels. It has long been thought that she sensed the vibrations of the ship's engine or of the sounding whistle. Another plausible theory is that since Patsy Ann would mostly hang out at the longshoremen's hall, she would simply notice them leaving to meet the ship and follow along. But no one is really sure how she did it.

One story people love to tell is the time that the local newspaper mistakenly published the wrong dock that a ship would be arriving at. As the ship approached, people lined up and waited at the wrong spot. As Patsy Ann came down to greet the ship, she glanced over at the mistaken crowd and then ambled over to another dock. When the arriving ship proved that Patsy Ann alone had chosen the correct dock the people marveled as to how the little dog could have possibly known.

She died peacefully while sleeping at the longshoremen's hall, March 30, 1942. She was buried at sea the next day along the waterfront when her coffin was lowered into the Gastineau Channel. Years later the "Friends of Patsy Ann" commissioned New Mexico sculptor, Anna Harris, to create a life size bronze statue. It was unveiled in July, 1992 on the waterfront where she keeps a watchful eye toward the incoming ships. If you ever go to Juneau you can read her story on the plaque, pet her or playfully make believe she bit off your finger, but she'll just sit there gazing out to sea and waiting for the next ship to roll in so she can say hello.

Patsy Ann continues to be a famous character. Tourists enjoy the statue and take lots of pictures. The Gastineau Humane Society receives letters from around the world wanting to hear the story of the loveable dog and her statue. She has been the subject of a few short books and her legend lives on.

ENJOYING SOME SUNSHINE WHILE WAITING FOR HER SHIP TO COME IN.

In a travel article about Alaska that appeared in the New York Times May 30, 1937, the writer penned a first-hand account of the little dog while she was still alive. I think it captures Patsy Ann's charm in a pleasant way. In an article titled "ALASKA, WHERE LIFE IS MERRY "-"Rare Sense of Humor" the writer penned the following:

> *Akin to the sporting spirit of the North is the sense of humor, the complete lack of self-consciousness evidenced in Alaskan communities. For example, Juneau, the capital and largest city, does not have a Chamber of Commerce delegation to meet distinguished arrivals. The official greeter for the city, so attested by a handsome, gold-plated collar, is a rheumy-eyed, unbelievably scrawny old white dog named Patsy Ann. Stone–deaf, Patsy's ears are attuned only to the vibrations of a steamboat whistle. Then she lopes to the wharf to howl in F minor beneath the galley porthole and blink a watery greeting to the throng crowding down the gangplank.*

How could you not love a dog like that?

MONUMENT ON THE JUNEAU WHARF

Credit: Noel Price–2012

CHAPTER 14

IGLOO

He was more than a friend.

—Admiral Richard Byrd

Perhaps the greatest and most famous adventurer of the twentieth century was Rear Admiral Richard Byrd. Besides many other accomplishments, he was the first man to fly over both the North and South Poles. His expeditions to the Polar Regions were truly complex, dangerous and amazing voyages. And by his side was a good looking alert white dog that he grew to cherish and who lifted his master's spirits during the darkest hours of their long challenging journeys together. His name was Igloo, and just to look at him and watch his antics was guaranteed to put a smile on your face.

On a dark cold night in the winter of 1926 a little white dog with brown ears sought shelter in a storefront in Washington, DC. A nice lady took pity on the young vagrant and took him home with her. She warmed him up, washed and fed him. He was a sturdy, eager to please, wire fox terrier that had a way of making you like him. Since she could not keep him where she lived, she wondered what to do.

IGLOO

Ohio State University–Byrd Polar Research Center

Lieutenant Commander Richard E. Byrd of the U.S. Navy was making a name for himself as a world known explorer. He had just returned from an adventure in Greenland. He was now busy preparing and loading his ship, the Chantier, and was soon to depart for his base in Norway, where he would attempt to be first to fly over the North Pole. The newspapers were alive with stories of competing adventurers in a race north. In 1909, Captain Robert E. Peary had been credited with being the first to stand over the Pole, but now we had airplanes and it was a chance for someone to have the notoriety of being the first by air.

Miss Boggs, the lady with the dog, read the stories and remembered that she had once met the Lieutenant Commander. She thought it would be a great idea to give him the dog to take along on his trip. She contacted him and despite his initial resistance to the idea, she persistently made her case and he finally agreed. The dog was delivered and came aboard the ship in a crate. He was given the name Igloo by Byrd and soon called 'Iggy' for short. He soon worked his way out of the crate and into Byrd's heart and in no time at all he was living in his master's room and curling up on his bed. He quickly discovered that being the Commander's dog was the way to go in life. Iggy seemed to sense the benefits of his new position, and ever after trotted around with a sense of authority and entitlement.

When the Chantier was ready, they set sail for Spitsbergen, Norway, the base for the polar flight attempt. On the voyage across the Atlantic, Commander Byrd became better acquainted with his new companion's personality. As with most intelligent beings he was very curious. Once he got settled in, Igloo took to exploring the ship and soon discovered the ship's cat, Shipwreck. They met unexpectedly when Shipwreck pounced on the unsuspecting dog and sent him running for cover. On their next meeting Igloo was ready for battle and this time he held his own. After these two tussles they seemed to grudgingly tolerate each other's presence and peace onboard was restored. Upon arrival at the base Igloo was taken ashore and discovered he loved to play in the deep snow. He would run in circles, burrow and roll around enjoying the fluffy powder. His ability to tolerate and even enjoy snow and ice would serve him well in the next few years.

The airplane to be used on the historic flight was taken ashore, assembled and preparations were hurriedly made. Several other explorers were racing to beat them. The Norwegian explorer Roald Amundson was based at the same location preparing for his own aerial attempt. He was waiting for his dirigible, the Norge, to arrive from Italy. It was a friendly competition with each team wishing the other good luck. Amundson was an experienced and worthy rival. On December 14, 1911 he had accomplished an amazing feat when he became the first man to reach the South Pole, beating British explorer Richard Scott by a month.

On May 9th Byrd, acting as navigator, and his good friend and pilot Floyd Bennet made what was claimed to be the first flight over the North Pole. They flew from their base in Spitsbergen and back in 15.5 hours. They had just barely beaten the other teams. Three days later Amundson passed over the pole in the Norge. Upon their return by way of London and on to New York the team and Byrd were shocked by the crowds waiting to see them. The press took notice of the Commander's photogenic canine companion and he became part of the story. Byrd received the Congressional Medal of Honor for his triumph.

After the excitement died down they returned to the Commander's home in Boston and Igloo settled into a brief period of family life. He learned to play with the children and enjoyed walks along the waterfront with his master. Byrd stayed busy; this was an exciting era of aviation firsts. In fact, he helped tutor Charles Lindbergh in navigation skills before his historic non-stop solo flight in 1927 across the Atlantic. Lindbergh also came to know Igloo and enjoyed his charming company. Byrd followed up Lindbergh's flight with his own aviation feat a few weeks later. He and three companions also flew across the Atlantic in a recorded time of 42 hours. For that feat he received the French Legion of Honor.

In 1928 Commander Byrd announced that he was launching a mission to explore the Antarctic frontier. With temperatures that had been recorded at 130 degrees below zero, the hostile environment had halted previous exploration attempts and most of the continent remained a mystery. Byrd launched his first Antarctic expedition (he completed four more in his lifetime) when his expedition sailed south from New York City on August 25, 1928. Their ship, a bark named the City of New York was accompanied by the auxiliary supply ship, the Eleanor Bolling, on its 15,000 mile four month voyage. Byrd and Igloo traveled by train across the United States where they boarded a steamship in San Pedro, traveled across the Pacific and joined up with the expedition in New Zealand. From there they traveled to the Ross Ice Shelf to build their shelter and a base for their stay in what was considered the last unknown frontier on earth.

On this expedition a camera crew came along to record the action. Today we can watch the film "With Byrd at the South Pole" in the warmth of our 21st century living rooms and get a taste of and appreciate the harsh conditions that the crew faced. Igloo's antics helped put some levity into what was an incredibly difficult (physically and mentally) mission. In the film we see Igloo's inquisitive interactions with large and equally curious Emperor penguins. They eye each other without fear wondering what to do and what they are looking at. Igloo gets close to seals and even whales who surface to breathe through small gaps in the ice. We see our brave yet cautious little explorer get very close then scurry away when the whales spout in his direction. The days of dogs nosing up to penguins are now over in Antarctica as they are no longer permitted on the continent.

When they arrived at the chosen location on the Ross Ice Shelf, the crew went about the hard work of unloading the ship, bringing ashore the supplies, sleds, dogs and airplanes. They then began building their base, Little America, and setting up the radio towers

CITY OF NEW YORK IN ANTARCTICA

Ohio State University-Byrd Polar Research Center

IGLOO IN HIS SNOW SUIT

Ohio State University–Byrd Polar Research Center

IGLOO WITH HIS COMRADES

Ohio State University-Byrd Polar Research Center

IGLOO AND ADMIRAL BYRD IN ANTARCTICA

Ohio State University-Byrd Polar Research Center

they needed to communicate with the outside world. We see Igloo is always there running around in the background having a great time, barking encouragement.

The many sled dogs brought along for transportation were given shelters outside in the snow. They will face the subzero temperatures with the protection their breeding has provided. In the movie, we see them curled up covered with snow and eating chunks of meat thrown at them while chained to their individual boxes. Meanwhile; Igloo hangs out with the guys in their nice cozy barracks eating at the table with Byrd. Once again, being the Commander's dog pays off big time. The sled dogs would get a bit of revenge at times and Igloo sported many scars from his run-ins with these furry working team members.

While gathered in the living quarters you can see the smiles and delight in the men's eyes as they parade him on top of a table wearing the snow suit they custom tailored for him complete with four miniature dog boots. Igloo's comical appearance in the outfit caused a lot of laughter. It is obvious that the men really enjoyed his company which helped brighten the long winter's darkness. We also see Igloo lounging around contentedly watching Commander Byrd as he works at his desk. When he thought no one was watching, Igloo would secretly cache his dog biscuits at the bottom of the Commanders sleeping bag. How do you measure the value of such a delightful companion?

Igloo did spend a lot of time outside and it is said that he developed the thickest coat of fur ever seen in that breed of dog. Byrd became more and more attached to his loyal friend whose gay personality helped him battle the bouts of depression inevitably brought on by the long periods of darkness and confined living quarters. Preparing for the winter, the City of New York departed for New Zealand, leaving the men stranded to face the bitter cold alone. They were on their own for the next nine months without any hope of assistance in case of emergency. They hunkered down into their routine and waited as the temperature dropped. In the film, we see the men noting that at the same time that their temperature was a numbing minus 72 degrees it was 96 in New York, a difference of 168 degrees!

On April 19 the sun disappeared and would not return for 125 days. The long polar night had begun. All that the men could do was survive and wait for at least 7 months until they could accomplish the mission they had come to perform, flying over the South Pole. Many others who had come to Antarctica before them had perished and lost the war of the elements they were about to wage. The climate, loneliness and unavoidable monotony were their biggest challenges, yet they had what someone described as a "a little white bundle of noise" with a charming personality to help lift their spirits, Igloo.

Eventually, the sun returned and a grateful team of 42 men prepared for the historic mission ahead. On November 29, 1929 with Byrd as navigator and three other crew members the team accomplished the first flight over the South Pole. The dangerous journey over towering peaks took 19 hours to complete. Byrd used a sextant and compass to verify his position. He then threw out, as a marker, a small flag wrapped around a stone taken from his old friend and partner's (Floyd Bennet) grave. They had combined the relatively new inventions of the airplane, radios, and cameras with old fashioned ships and dogsleds to make significant scientific achievements. They mapped and gathered valuable new information about the previously mysterious continent. For his accomplishments, Byrd would be promoted to Rear Admiral. And Iggy was there for the whole adventure.

They returned as heroes to a world that had been following the Commander's and Igloo's accomplishments. They were happy to be back in the world of sunshine, greenery and people after nearly two years cutoff from civilization in the vast icebound wasteland. His contemporary explorers Scott, Shackleton, and Amundson all lost their lives in the Polar Regions, yet remarkably Byrd had accomplished his mission without the loss of a man. Upon their triumphant return to New York, Byrd and Igloo were huge celebrities and enjoyed one of

BYRD, SANTA CLAUS AND IGLOO

Courtesy of the Boston Public Library-Leslie Jones Collection

RECEPTION IN BOSTON

Ohio State University–Byrd Polar Research Center

the greatest receptions ever with a ticker tape parade down Broadway. Igloo even met and was petted by President Herbert Hoover. Igloo was living the good life. He was put up at the Biltmore Hotel and the Tail Waggers Club presented him with a gold medal and special certificate.

Eventually they returned home to Massachusetts where they enjoyed a special parade and were greeted as conquering heroes by their hometown of Boston. Igloo was soon thereafter returned to the calm of the family home, and a fun life with the Admiral's four children. It was quite a change for a dog who had participated in some of the most adventurous explorations in history.

While Byrd, the now very famous and much in demand explorer, was touring the country delivering speeches, word came that Igloo was very sick. Apparently the soft ways of civilization had not agreed with him. Byrd immediately canceled the tour to quickly return home to see his dying friend. The tour sponsors pleaded with him to reconsider reminding him that the audience included a U.S. Senator, Episcopal Bishop, the city Mayor, other politicians and a sold out auditorium. The Admiral was not swayed, his dog came first. Unfortunately, Igloo succumbed and on April 20, 1931 passed away. The Admiral was devastated. He wrote later that Igloo was a unique dog with "qualities of gaiety, intelligence and sympathy." He also remarked that "...the endless entertainment he gave to the men of our party in the Polar Regions was worth unmeasured gold."

Major newspapers carried the story and there was a public outpouring of grief. Admiral Byrd was delivered thousands of letters of sympathy from children around the world. Igloo never performed any heroic deeds and did not directly save any lives, but he touched many hearts, made a lot of friends and made people smile when they needed it most. A suitable monument and burial site were chosen and plans were made. It was decided to bury him in a dog sized white coffin with silver handles at the Pine Ridge Pet Cemetery in Dedham, Massachusetts. There is a headstone monument to him, in

IGLOO, BYRD'S DOG, POLAR HERO, IS DEAD

Mascot of Expeditions to Both Ends of the Earth Succumbs at Explorer's Boston Home.

ADMIRAL CALLED TOO LATE

He Had Canceled Lecture and Started East When Word Came of Loss of "More Than Friend."

Special to The New York Times.

BOSTON, Mass., April 21.—Igloo, the little white fox terrier that shared in the adventures of Rear Admiral Richard E. Byrd in the frozen wastes of both tips of the earth, is dead at the Admiral's home here on Brimmer Street.

NY TIMES APRIL 22, 1931

HEADSTONE AT PET CEMETERY

Courtesy of the Boston Public Library-Leslie Jones Collection

the shape of an iceberg, there today. When interviewed shortly after Igloo's death, Byrd remarked that "He was more than a friend."Those are the words on his headstone.

There is also a nice bronze life size statue of Byrd and Igloo located in front of the Winchester-Fredrick County Judicial Center in Virginia. They are sculpted together forever with the Admiral reaching down with his right hand to pet his loyal friend, Igloo.

MONUMENT IN VIRGINIA

Photo Credit: Craig Swain

CHAPTER 15

GELERT

Look before you leap...
—Samuel Butler

his story finds us surrounded by the beautiful scenery of Northern Wales in Snowdonia National Park. High mountains, wooded valleys and picturesque lakes dot the landscape. Beddgelert is one of the area's loveliest villages.

Here we find a monument to Gelert, a truly legendary dog. He was a large Wolfhound who belonged to Llywelyn the Great, Prince of Gwynedd. Gelert was a gift from King John of England.

It is one of history and literature's classic cases of tragically mistaken identity. Llywelyn returns home from hunting and is alarmed to find his baby missing. He is then greeted by his dog Gelert, whose face is covered in blood. Upset and horrified, he draws his sword and slays the canine murderer. Gelert lets out a dying yelp as his master's sword pierces him. The baby, who is unharmed, but hidden under the cradle, lets out a cry at the same time. As Llywelyn runs to the child he also

THE ILLUSTRATION OF THE LEGEND

finds a dead wolf. He suddenly realizes the truth; Gelert had killed the attacking wolf while defending the baby. Filled with remorse he buries his heroic pet with great ceremony and it is said that he never smiled again.

It certainly is a heart wrenching tale, and a great lesson for all of us to not jump to conclusions, but historians tell us that Gelert may have never existed.

Different versions of the story are found throughout the world with a few cultural variations, depending on where it is told. From the Alpine region of Europe we hear about a shepherd who kills his sheepdog after finding a dead carcass and the blood covered dog. Later he finds a dead wolf in the stable and realizes his mistake. In Malaysian folklore, a hunter's tame pet bear is left to guard the house and his daughter. When the hunter returns home, the daughter is missing and the bear covered in blood. He kills the bear with his spear but later finds a dead tiger, which had been killed by the bear. His daughter then emerges from the jungle where she had been hiding during the struggle.

This mistake of assessing the facts, jumping to conclusions, and taking an action that seems to be justified but ultimately turns out to be incorrect is a theme that is found in many other stories. One is accused based on what seems to be conclusive evidence, and it is later discovered that there is a reasonable explanation after all. It is a lesson we all need to remember. There is a nice memorial in Beddgelert with two slate stones over the grave. One is inscribed in Welsh and the other in English. It reads as follows:

In the 13th Century, LLywelyn, Prince of North Wales, had a palace at Beddgelert. One day he went hunting without Gelert, "the faithful hound" who was unaccountably absent. On Llywelyn's return, the truant stained and smeared with blood, joyfully sprang to meet his master. The Prince, alarmed, hastened to find his son, and saw the infant's cot empty. The bedclothes and floor covered

GELERT'S GRAVESITE

Photo credit: Rob Lindsey

*with blood. The frantic father plunged the sword into the hound's
side, thinking it had killed his heir.*

*The dog's dying yell was answered by a child's cry. Llywelyn
searched and discovered his boy unharmed, but nearby lay the body
of a mighty wolf which Gelert had slain. The Prince filled with
remorse is said never to have smiled again. He buried Gelert here.
The spot is called Beddgelert.*

This type of story is classified as a classic contemporary legend,
and is a variation on the "faithful hound" folk-tale motif. It is a famous
story, and there are many fine poems based on it. I have copied one
below. I think is a tale worth hearing, and who knows, maybe it is
true after all.

So the next time you see some poor cartoon dog with feathers
around his mouth get whacked by Granny, because Tweety is missing,
but it was really Sylvester who was after the bird, which the poor dog
had stepped in to defend. Remember the story of Gelert.

BETH GELERT
The Grave of the Greyhound

*The spearman heard the bugle sound,
And cheerily smiled the morn;
And many a brach, and many a hound,
Attend Llewellyn's horn:*

*And still he blew a louder blast,
And gave a louder cheer:
"Come, Gelert! Why art thou last
Llewellyn's horn to hear?"*

"Oh, where does faithful Gelert roam?

The flower of all his race!
So true, so brave, a lamb at home,
A lion in the chase!"

In sooth, he was a peerless hound,
The gift of royal John,
But now no Gelert could be found
And all the chase rode on.

And now, as over rocks and dells,
The gallant chidings rise,
All Snowdon's craggy chaos yells
With many mingled cries.

That day Llewellyn little loved
The chase of hart or hare,
And small and scant the booty proved,
For Gelert was not there.

Unpleased, Llewellyn homeward hied,
When near the portal-seat,
His truant Gelert he espied,
Bounding his lord to meet.

But when he gained the castle door,
Aghast the chieftain stood;
The hound was smeared with gouts of gore,
His lips and fangs ran blood.

Llewellyn gazed with wild surprise,
Unused such looks to meet;
His favorite checked his joyful guise,
And crouched and licked his feet.

Onward in haste Llewellyn passed,

And on went Gelert, too,
And still, where'er his eyes were cast,
Fresh blood-gouts shocked his view.

O'erturned his infant's bed he found,
The blood stained cover rent;
And all around, the walls and ground,
With recent blood besprent.

He called the child—no voice replied;
He searched, with terror wild;
Blood! Blood! He found on every side,
But nowhere found the child!

"Hell-hound! By thee my child's devoured!"
The frantic father cried;
And to the hilt his vengeful sword
He plunged in Gelert's side.

His suppliant, as to earth he fell,
No pity could impart,
But still his Gelert's dying yell
Pass heavy o'er his heart.

Aroused by Gelert's dying yell,
Some slumberer wakened nigh;
What words the parent's joy can tell
His hurried search had missed,
All glowing from his rosy sleep,
His cherub-boy he kissed.

No scratch had he, nor harm, nor dread,
But, the same couch beneath,
Lay a great wolf, all torn and dead—
Tremendous still in death.

Ah! What was then Llewellyn's pain!
For now the truth was clear:
The gallant hound the wolf had slain
To save Llewellyn's heir.

Van, vain was all Llewellyn's woe;
"Best of thy kind, adieu!
The frantic deed which laid thee low
This heart shall ever rue!"

And now a gallant tomb they raise,
With costly sculpture decked,
And marbles, storied with his praise,
Poor Gelert's bones protect.

Here never could the spearman pass,
Or forester, unmoved!
Here oft the tear-besprinkled grass
Llewellyn's sorrow proved.

And here he hung his horn and spear,
And oft, as evening fell,
In fancy's piercing sounds would hear
Poor Gelert's dying yell.
—William Robert Spencer c. 1800

CHAPTER 16

OLD DRUM

Man's Best Friend

The year was 1869 near the town of Warrensburg, Missouri. It had barely been 4 years since the end of the Civil War. The war and the years preceding had been very hard on this part of the country. The Union and especially the State of Missouri had been divided philosophically and as a result neighbors and even families had been torn apart. There had been too much violence and turmoil and now life was returning to normal. Farms and families were beginning to be productive once again and it looked like the worst was now thankfully behind them.

The hero and inspiration for our next story is a black and tan hunting dog named Old Drum. His owner named him Drum because that was what he sounded like when he got to barking. By most accounts he was one of the fastest and best hunting hounds in that neck of the woods. He does not live long into the tale but he is there in the background the whole time.

~

George Graham Vest

Old Drum, his favorite dog was missing. After failing to come home the night before, his owner Charles Burden went out and began his search. Charles found him lying lifeless near Big Creek. He had been shot. There was no direct evidence but all the circumstances pointed to his neighbor and brother-in law as being the cause of the dog's demise.

Leonidas Hornsby suspected that his neighbor's hound dog was the varmint who had been killing his animals. He was trying to run a farm but something had been decimating his livestock, mostly the sheep. He suspected local dogs might be part of the problem. He had let it be known publically that he would shoot the next dog he saw on his property.

Hornsby admitted that he had indeed instructed his nephew to shoot at a marauding dog the night before, but insisted that it was a different dog, not Old Drum, and besides that, they had loaded the shotgun with dried corn so it was unlikely that they had killed anything.

Burden was unconvinced, but instead of taking the law into his own hands he opted to take it to court and filed a lawsuit for damages against his neighbor Hornsby. He did not intend to let the crime go unpunished. The heartfelt loss of his dog was the impetus for the historic events that soon unfolded. What followed was a court case that is still talked about today.

After several trials and appeals in the lower courts the case eventually worked its way up through the legal system to the final battle at the Johnson County Courthouse. Both sides were determined to win and each party was represented by high powered attorneys. The lawyers involved in the case would all go on to considerable success in the years following the trial. Burden's attorney George Vest stated that he would "win the case or apologize to every dog in Missouri."

Representing the defendant was the legal team of Tom Crittenden and Francis Cockrell. Crittenden had fought for the Union as a lieutenant colonel, and toward the end of the war had served as

Attorney General. In the years following the trial he went on to
serve as the Governor of Missouri. Cockrell had risen to the rank of
Brigadier General in the Confederate Army. He went on to serve as
a United States Senator for 5 terms and later served in the Roosevelt
administration.

On the other side for the Plaintiff were two lawyers who go on
to equally impressive records. John Phillips had been a Colonel in
the Union Army and later served on the federal bench as a judge for
twenty-two years. George Graham Vest had aligned himself with the
Confederate States of America and had served in the Confederate
Congress and Senate. Years after the trial, he was voted into the United
States Senate and served for twenty-four years. During his tenure he
is credited with saving Yellowstone National Park and fighting for
reform in the treatment of Native Americans.

Both sets of attorneys made their arguments before the court
and Judge Foster Wright. This would be the fourth and final trial.
The courtroom was packed. Testimony was given and depositions
from witnesses that now lived in other states were read as evidence.
The defense argued that indeed a dog was shot but that it was a
different dog and someone else must have shot Drum. Burden said
that Old Drum was the best dog he had ever owned, Hornsby was
responsible for his death, and that he deserved to be compensated for
his loss. On September 23, 1870, George Vest presented the following
closing remarks for Burden and Old Drum. His remarks are why we
remember the case today;

> *"The best friend a man has in the world may turn against him
> and become his enemy. His son or daughter that he has reared with
> loving care may prove ungrateful. Those who are nearest and dearest to
> us, those whom we trust with our happiness and our good name may
> become traitors to their faith. The money that a man has, he may lose. It
> flies away from him, perhaps when he needs it most. A man's reputation
> may be sacrificed in a moment of ill-considered action. The people who*

OLD JOHNSON COUNTY COURTHOUSE–WARRENSBURG, MISSOURI

are prone to fall on their knees to do us honor when success is with us may be the first to throw the stone of malice when failure settles its cloud upon our heads.

The one absolutely unselfish friend that man can have in this selfish world, the one that never deserts him, the one that never proves ungrateful or treacherous is his dog. A man's dog stands by him in prosperity and in poverty, in health and in sickness. He will sleep on the cold ground, where the wintry winds blow and the snow drives fiercely, if only he may be near his master's side. He will kiss the hand that has no food to offer; he will lick the wounds and sores that come in an encounter with the roughness of the world. He guards the sleep of his pauper master as if he were a prince. When all other friends desert, he remains. When riches take wings, and reputation falls to pieces, he is as constant in his love as the sun in its journey through the heavens.

If fortune drives the master forth an outcast in the world, friendless and homeless, the faithful dog asks no higher privilege than that of accompanying him, to guard him against danger, to fight against his enemies. And when the last scene of all comes, and death takes his master in its embrace and his body is laid away in the cold ground, no matter if all other friends pursue their way, there by the graveside will the noble dog be found, his head between his paws, his eyes sad, but open in alert watchfulness, faithful and true even in death."

This eloquent speech, which did not in any way allude to the facts or arguments in the case, was so impressive that when the jury's verdict was reached, the defendant was indeed found guilty and Burden was awarded his $50. In the end the case was about much more than the value of a dog but about a very important and vital piece of a man's life that had been thoughtlessly taken away. The defendant was guilty of killing the plaintiff's most precious possession, his pride and joy, his loyal friend and companion, his dog.

The case is still discussed and talked about today. The Missouri State archives provide documents and course materials to secondary schools in the state so that students can study and discuss the case, the people involved, and the famous eulogy. Was the circumstantial evidence sufficient? Did the powerful oration sway the court emotionally and cause facts to be ignored? Students can view the original court documents and discuss whether or not they think Hornsby was indeed guilty.

On the positive side the parties to the action remained neighbors and there is no record of any lingering animosity. They were neighbors and related by marriage, they had hunted together and Hornsby always had admired Old Drum for his hunting skills. They both paid a dear financial price but apparently they eventually recovered and lived peacefully. It certainly was a victory for the rule of law over the gun.

The old courthouse still stands and is used today as a museum for the Johnson County Historical Society. A plaque commemorating Vest's speech stands at the entrance. Today there is a nice statue of Old Drum in front of the current Johnson County Courthouse in Warrensburg, Missouri. It has a plaque with the entire "Tribute to the Dog" written on it. There is another monument placed on the banks of the Big Creek near where the body of Drum was found. It contains the inscription:

Killed, Old Drum, 1869

The speech has lived on and is a pleasant example of the orator's art. The power of the spoken word to sway opinion and stir human emotion is well documented and continues today. As an example of the enduring fame of the speech consider the following; on February 6th, 1925, after the successful serum run to Nome, the United States Senate set aside other business and allowed Senator Dill of Washington to pay tribute to the men and dogs that were the heroes of that drama. As part of his tribute he entered into the congressional record George Vest's 'Eulogy of the Dog.' Fifty-five years after it had been delivered in faraway Missouri, it was still talked about and considered a great speech.

STATE HISTORICAL MARKER–OWENSBORO, KENTUCKY

OLD DRUM'S MONUMENT–WARRENSBURG, MISSOURI

Some even consider it one of the greatest speeches ever given, comparing it with Patrick Henry's *Give me Liberty or give me Death*, Jesus's *Sermon on the Mount*, Lincoln's *Gettysburg Address* and other famous orations. William Safire, noted journalist, speech writer and language expert, considered and listed Vest's 'Eulogy of the Dog' as one of the best speeches of all time. Vest later put his oratory skills to good use during his years in the U.S. Senate. His speech is credited with originating the expression that "A man's best friend is his dog."

It really is a touching and powerful speech and the words chosen and their rhythm speaks to the heart, but it is the subject that sets it above and apart from other speeches. The dog, man's faithful companion since the Stone Age on a journey through a cold dark universe, our best friend.

Acknowledgements

I wish to thank all the nice people and institutions who helped.

Chapter 1- Greyfriars Bobby

Peter Stubbs –Photographer- www.edinphoto.org.uk
Denise Brace-Curator History-The Museum of Edinburgh

Chapter 2-Barry

Dr. Marc Nussbaumer-Natural History Museum Bern, Switzerland

Chapter 3-Sergeant Stubby

Kathy Golden-National Museum of American History- Associate
Curator, Smithsonian Institution Washington DC
Kay Peterson-Archives Center-Smithsonian Institution
Edward C Martin III Vice-President-Hartsdale Pet Cemetery-
Hartsdale, New York

Chapter 4-Rin Tin Tin

Dorothy Yanchak
Rin Tin Tin, www.RinTinTin.com
Kevin Hallaran-Riverside Metropolitan Museum

Chapter 5-Dog on the Tuckerbox

Cindy Smith-Gundagai Library – Gundagai NSW, Australia
Ned Lewis-Denny Events & Retail Coordinator

Chapter 6-Hachi-ko

Akira Fukui-National Museum of Nature and Science- Tokyo, Japan
Gail Sumpter-Photographer

Chapter 7–Bobbie
Amy Platt–*The Oregon Encyclopedia*
Dave Crockett
Susan Stelljes– www.Silvertonbobbie.com
Chris Schwab–Silverton Country Historical Society
Jan Wolford long–Silverton Country Historical Society
Scott Rook–Oregon Historical Society
Kathrin Sumpter–Photographer

Chapter 8–Waghya
Sandeep Kamble– www.raigad-fort.info
Amit Kulkarni– http://amitkulkarni.info/pics/

Chapter 9–Balto & Togo
Glenda Bogar –Cleveland Museum of Natural History
Wendy Wasman–Cleveland Museum of Natural History
James O'Donnell– Smithsonian National Postal Museum
Patrice Hamiter–Cleveland Public Library
Mary E. Montgomery–Museum of History & Industry–Seattle
Kathleen Kennedy–Museum of History & Industry–Seattle
Carol Butler–Brown Brothers
Sandra Johnson–Alaska State Library

Chapter 10–Owney
James O'Donnell–Smithsonian National Postal Museum

Chapter 11–Swansea Jack
Ivor Williams–Treboeth History Society–Wales
Beverley Cuddy–Tailwaggers Club Trust

Chapter 12–Bamse
Dr. Andrew Orr– Co-Author– *"Sea Dog Bamse-World War II Canine Hero"*-Chairman-Montrose Heritage Trust-Scotland

Chapter 13–Patsy Ann
Sandra Johnson–Alaska State Library
Noel Price –Photographer

Chapter 14–Igloo
Craig Swain–Photographer
Laura Kissel-Byrd Polar Research Center Archival Program
– Columbus Ohio
Jane Winton–Boston Public library

Chapter 15–Gelert
Rob Lindsey-Photographer

Special Thanks

Phil Tauran Photography
Matt Morolla-Photograher
Marina Shipova
Gail Sumpter
Kathrin Sumpter

Afterthoughts

Writing this book was an interesting journey and a rewarding experience. I already knew quite a bit about most of my subjects, but as I uncovered and learned more details, my admiration for the dogs grew. The story locations and historical backdrops were also pleasant discoveries. The interaction of our dogs with events such as world wars, heroic explorations, railroad mail service, and the cinema, all go to show that like man, no dog is an island.

Most of the stories are touching and some are hard to believe. I am blown away by the story of Silverton Bobbie. The drive and ability to find his way home from so far away is absolutely amazing. I was able to communicate with the people who still breed the descendants of Rin Tin Tin. That dog turned out to be by all accounts a very special dog indeed. He had quite a life and deserves all the attention he was given. What a beautiful dog.

I think my favorite character has to be Igloo. Saving lives is great, but if you are going to be holed up for months and months in the freezing dark, a friendly comical companion is indeed worth his weight in gold.

I could not have written the book without the internet. I was able to communicate quickly with people and institutions in Texas, Norway, Japan, Switzerland, Australia, Alaska, Wales, Washington, DC, Ohio, Massachusetts and even India all while sitting here in my office in Sequim, Washington. It was reassuring that people were so pleasant and helpful. It has been a lot of fun. Thank you to everyone who took the time to talk to me, answer my e-mails, and send me information and for wishing me success on my project. They all had one thing in common and reaffirmed what I have always known to be true; people who love dogs are nice people.

Thank you to everyone.

Let me know which story is your favorite. Have you heard a

'monumental dog' story that I should know about? Write to me and let me know. I would love to hear from you.

Ed Sumpter/Sequim, Washington
edseds@olypen.com

About the Author

Ed Sumpter lives in Sequim, Washington, near the edge of the beautiful Olympic National Park. Ed is currently the owner of Blue Sky Real Estate. He lives with his family and their best friend, Chief.